What people are saying about
Davy Meets His Goliath

"I enjoyed reading this book ~~because~~ it reminded me
of how important it is to treat other~~s~~  be treated. Have you ever gotten bu~~llied?~~
haven't gotten bullied, but I have se~~en~~
a mean thing to see. We all need to treat people with
respect and reach out to those we see being mistreated."

Jacob C. age 10

"*Davy Meets His Goliath* is an excellent short story
for kids that directly addresses the subject of bullying. More
than that, it invites the child as well as an adult, teacher,
parent, etc. to open a meaningful dialogue on some of the
causes and effects of being bullied. Beyond that, there
are worksheets included that allow children to express
their feelings on being bullied and to discuss reasons on
why it may occur, ways to deal with it, and how to help
others get through the experience. It also suggests ways to
try and prevent it from happening to them or others
around them. *Davy meets his Goliath* is an easy and
interesting read, and I would recommend it as required
reading to all elementary school children and teachers."

Alan Jude Summa/ Illustrator-Author

"The story is wonderful. The conversation it brings is essential for not only kids but also adults. Bullying is certainly a problem for young people, but it is also something that happens to adults. The story leads people to a conversation on how to handle bullying. We need to practice the steps of how to handle difficult situations. I was a big fan of practicing difficult situations with my children and modeling how to handle themselves when unpleasantness happens.

This story provides a model on how to walk through the steps of conflict. Most importantly, the story models that we need to ask for help."

Rachel Gilbert/ Teacher, former K-12 Social Studies Coordinator for Abington Heights School District and Mother of Four

"One of the best methods to capture your audience and teach a lesson is through a story. The greatest Teacher used this method to reveal deep truths, and still does today.

"*Davy Meets His Goliath* is a powerful tool for parents and teachers. James uses a story to discuss a sensitive topic to today's kids. This book has helped us guide our children into a conversation about how to navigate relationships, treating others the way we want to be treated, how to stand up for yourself and others, and when to elicit the help of adults.

"The powerful theme of trusting God to work in our lives and how the support from family and friends can encourage children to make good choices is evident in the pages of this book. Thanks for the resource, James!"

Laura Decker

"I like the way Davy talked to his parents." -Emily D., age 9

"Best way to tackle your enemies." -Henry D., age 11

"James has written a book to capture a child's heart. Readers, no matter their age, will see themselves in Davy's story. Parents and teachers will appreciate the guided questions to help their young readers navigate the topic of bullying. Great for classrooms and family rooms, but a MUST READ for anyone who has ever dealt with bullying, loneliness, and making new friends."

Melissa Zabower/ author of *In the Shadow of Mr. Lincoln*

"*Davy Meets his Goliath* is an excellent book for young people, parents, schools, and practitioners about the importance of kindness, the impact of bullying, making wise choices and changes, the principle of forgiveness, and personal growth.

"Written in age-appropriate language, both younger children and teenagers will benefit from its contents. The thought-provoking questions at the end of each chapter will help the reader explore chapter contents and provide further insight on the topic. At the end of the book is a helpful parent guide to assist parents with book contents.

"The book is written from a Christian perspective, including Bible verses; however, it can be applied to all faith perspectives. Also, from a therapeutic standpoint, **Davy Meets his Goliath** is an excellent addition to a therapist's toolbox."

Kara B. Golden/ MSW, LCSW

Davy Meets His Goliath

A book written by

James

AUTHENTIC ENDEAVORS
PUBLISHING
www.AuthenticEndeavorsPublishing.com

www.DavyMeetsHisGoliath.com

www.DavyMeetsHisGoliath.com
www.TogetherWeCanEndBullying.com

Authentic Endeavors Publishing
Clarks Summit PA 18411
© 2020 Illustrated by Alan Jude Summa & Laura Fleming
Summa
Cover Design by Alan Jude Summa & Laura Fleming Summa
Interior design by Bethany Shaffer

ISBN: 978-0-9982105-4-4

Dedication

This book is dedicated to children who live their lives in fear of being picked on by others — children who lose trust and self-worth because of this very same cause, may they find shelter from their fear. And also to the hurting souls that find bullying to be an outlet for their anger and frustration in dealing with their issues, may they find resolve and forgiveness and come to an understanding that anger cures no pain and love can heal all wounds.

So many children in our communities have been bullied or are part of bullying all through our schools, in various social settings, in sports, and even worse still online through social media.

May they all find peace knowing that there is a light at the end of this darkness and that light is the truth and love received in the word of God.

Acknowledgments

I want to take this time to acknowledge the Student Ministry group of Parker Hill Church. Without the dedication and drive for the work they do to represent the teachings of our Lord and Savior, Jesus Christ, this story may not have been told.

Special thanks and much gratitude to Laura Decker, who saw something in me, which prompted an invitation for me to become a small group leader in the church's student ministry. My acceptance of that invitation and participation in that ministry has forever changed my life. Laura is a blessing and inspiration. I hope others will follow her lead, revealing the passion they have to pass on to this and the next generation of God's children the importance of living a life dedicated to serving the God who created us all.

In advance, to all the parents and student ministry groups around the globe, that will use this story to teach the love of God to our youth and to spread the good news that love is mightier than hate and forgiveness is possible for all of us with the help of our loving God. May you all be blessed in his presence and do wonderful work in his name.

And, most importantly, I want to thank God for giving me the privilege of delivering this beautiful story. God bless you

Table of Contents

Table of Contents

Leader and Parent Guide

Foreword

Danny Howard

Student Ministries Pastor

More and more students today are living in a world full of pressures and challenges which come in all shapes and sizes and know no age boundaries. At times those pressures can be unrealistic and unmet expectations, academic challenges, or many other things. Far too often, the challenges our students face today come at the hands of a peer.

As a parent, I believe the content delivered in this book will open the door to better communication with your children. Often, it can be challenging for a student to know when and even how to talk to his or her parents about the pressures they are facing. But the tools that James has given in this book, I believe, will really help to open those lines of communication.

In my time as a teacher, and now as a Student Ministries Pastor, I have seen bullying affect many of the social settings our children are a part of today. In the time I have known James, it is very easy for me to see that he has a heart and a passion for students who are dealing with these pressures. As you read through the pages of this story, it will be easy for you to see this and his convictions.

James has not only chosen to write a story for kids to read and enjoy but has given parent/leader guides that will be great for a family discussion or a group study. I love his passion that is evident in this engaging story, as well as taking it another step by giving tools to help with the application of what the readers are learning to apply to their own unique situations. The questions are designed to promote open conversation by helping to build confidence and deeper relationships with God, their parents, the leaders they look to for support, and their peers.

This book reinforces that a child doesn't need to feel alone in any situation. God is always with them, and they can ask Him for help, as Davy learns to do throughout the story.

Enjoy

Chapter One

Sometimes Things Can Be Unexpected

"Can you believe there's only one more day of school left?" Davy said with excitement. "We're going to have the whole summer to do whatever we want!"

"Yeah, maybe we can start building that fort now!" said Jimmy.

"What about the flag football league we're going to start? I can't wait to pick teams!" chimed in Cooper.

School had just let out for the day. Davy and his friends, Jimmy and Cooper, walked home together, as they often did. Every time they walked, they would dream up fun ideas and things to do together. You could tell the boys were like brothers by their laughter and light-hearted banter. Since the last day of school was only a day away, they were happily making their plans for summer. Having fun during summer break was at the top of their list of

www.DavyMeetsHisGoliath.com

things to do, and it would start as soon as the last bell of the school year rang.

Davy lived closest to school. Jimmy lived just two houses down, and Cooper lived on the next block, just behind Jimmy's house. When they arrived at Davy's house, they discovered his mom, dad, and little sister, Susie, on the porch. The boys said their goodbyes and were on their way.

As Davy walked up the driveway, his dad shouted with a lively voice, "Come on, Davy, I have some great news I want to share with everyone!"

So, Davy hurried the rest of the way home. Just as they all sat down at the kitchen table together, his dad popped back to his feet, threw his hands in the air, and made his big announcement.

"I got it! I got it! I got the new job I put in for, and they asked me to start right away!"

Mom jumped up, gave Dad a big hug, and shouted, "Congratulations, Honey, I'm so proud of you! We'll be able to get that new house we've been dreaming about. Oh, my goodness. God has answered our prayers!"

Later that night, after things settled down, and it was time for bed, Davy laid his head down and started to pray. "Why? Why now, God? I've just made summer plans with my friends. I don't understand. Why do I have to leave now?"

As he closed his eyes to fall asleep, Davy felt a little sad knowing he was going to miss his friends and doing all the fun stuff they had planned to do together over the summer. He was looking forward to building a fort and playing flag football with his best friends. Although there might be time to do some of what the boys had planned, Davy would be moving in the middle of the summer. His parents were sure to leave enough time to pack for the move and for everyone to get settled into their new home before school started for Davy and Susie.

After a few weeks had gone by, it was the night before moving day. Davy wasn't very happy because he didn't want to leave his friends behind again. You see, Davy and his family had moved once before, and now that he was almost ten, Davy seemed to have more friends to miss, and he wasn't looking forward to trying to find new ones.

As he thought about leaving his friends, Davy was feeling sad. Remembering that it had taken him a while to get to know Jimmy and Cooper, he wondered, *"how in the world will I ever find such a friend as Jimmy. He's a lot of fun and has some really cool stuff for boys to play with. And*

Cooper, no one can throw a football as far as he can." After a while, Davy finally drifted off to sleep.

Morning came, and it was time to pack the truck and get ready to leave. After all their hard work of carefully packing, every box was neatly placed on the moving truck. Before long they were ready to go, and it was time for Davy to say goodbye to his buddies one last time. The three friends gave their secret handshake and then huddled together in a big group hug.

After what seemed to be a blur of a morning, the moving truck pulled out of the driveway and began down the road. And just like that, Davy was looking out the back window of his dad's car. As they drove past Jimmy's house, the two boys waved. Davy watched as they got farther and farther away. He smiled, thinking about his two friends, and just then, he realized it was time to look forward. He began to look forward to his new house, his new neighborhood and focused on the new adventures he and his family would have once they got settled into the new place his parents found for them.

"*Yes,*" he thought to himself. "*This is going to be all right, after all. Sure I'm going to miss those guys, but things are going to be all right. I'm going to be just fine.*"

As his faith in God grew, Davy started to feel more
relaxed about what was to come from this move and all the
possibilities in store for him.

Summer seemed to go by so fast while Davy and his
family were settling into their new home. Together they
made it feel all nice and cozy. They were really enjoying the
new neighborhood. Just down the road from their house
was a park that Davy and his sister went to all the time. It
had a nice playground with swings and a really big slide
that Davy liked. It was super fast! He went down the slide

www.DavyMeetsHisGoliath.com

over and over again. Susie really liked the merry-go-round, especially when Dad pushed! She got so dizzy it made her giggle.

Their new school was just a couple blocks past the park, so it was pretty easy for them to get around having everything close to home. Everything seemed to be going pretty smoothly.

Only a few days of summer break were left before school started. Davy couldn't help but wonder, "*What will it be like starting over in this new school? What will the kids be like? Will I be able to make new friends like the ones I had at my other school?*"

He often thought about his friends, Jimmy and Cooper, and wondered how their summer had gone. He did message them here and there and talked on the phone a couple of times to stay in touch, but it just wasn't the same as being there. He learned that Jimmy and Cooper built the fort they had planned to build. With some help from Jimmy's dad, it came out way better than they'd hoped. And the summer flag football league? Yep! Cooper and his team won the championship! The trophy was an old football, spray-painted gold, and stuck on a piece of wood that was leftover from building their fort. Davy laughed out loud when he learned about that one.

"*Those guys were fun,*" he thought. Davy's thoughts about his friends and his previous school had him thinking more and more about what was to come in the next couple of days, as well as the school year that was just about to start.

So, here it was, the night before the first day of school, and Davy had everything in order. His plan was in place, complete with his alarm clock being set and his lunch being packed. "*These jitters in my belly couldn't get any bigger!*" He thought. "*It kind of feels like a monkey is trapped in there because it's jumping around so much! I should go to bed now before it gets too late.*"

Davy laid his head down as he started saying his prayers. He began by asking God that he and his little sister would have a good day at their new school and that he would find new friends who were just as nice as his friends, Jimmy and Cooper. He prayed he would fit in and learn his school work. He asked for everything to be very much as it had been when he was at his former school. Before he finished praying, he already began to feel better knowing that God would be with him and watch over him on his new journey.

And just like that, he fell asleep, resting peacefully.

Chapter One

Think it Over

How did Davy feel when he first found out he and his family were going to be moving away, and all his plans were going to change unexpectedly?

_____

_____

_____

_____

_____

How do you think you would feel if you were Davy?

_____

_____

How did Davy's attitude change as he watched his friends from the back window of his Dad's car?

_____

_____

_____

_____

_____

Do you think you can be like Davy?

_____

_____

How?

_____

_____

_____

_____

_____

<u>Scripture References</u>

Proverbs 3: 5-6

Trust in the Lord with all your heart and lean not on your own understanding; in all ways, submit to him, and he will make your paths straight.

Romans 8: 28

And we know that in all things God works for the good of those who love him, who have been called according to his purpose.

Chapter Two
A New Beginning

Morning arrived as the alarm rang out in Davy's bedroom. He opened his eyes, rubbed them a bit, and then he remembered, *"This is it. Today's the big day... the first day at my new school!"*

A little nervous and a little excited at the same time, Davy got out of bed, brushed his teeth, splashed some water on his face, fixed his hair, and began getting ready for the day. Davy liked to make his bed before he got dressed, so that's what he did. Then he picked out clothes from his closet and got dressed, tucked in his shirt, and took a peek in the mirror to see how he did. With a quick nod of approval, he went off to the kitchen for breakfast.

Davy's mom, dad, and little sister were already downstairs waiting for him. As he entered the kitchen, he could smell his absolute favorite breakfast. Pancakes!

"Good morning," said Davy's mom. "I made your

favorite banana pancakes! I thought this would get you off to a good start today."

Davy's face lit up as he put a couple of mom's famous banana pancakes on his plate and totally covered them with gooey maple syrup. He bowed his head and gave thanks. "Thank you, God, for my mom, and that she made my favorite pancakes. Thank you for the food you give us to eat, and will you please be with me today for my first day at this new school?"

When he finished, he couldn't help but gulp down those yummy sticky pancakes and soon found himself staring at an empty plate, and still feeling a little bit hungry inside. His mom gave him another pancake to make sure his belly was full for his big day.

Davy finished his breakfast, wiped his face clean, and called out to his sister, "Come on Susie, it's time to go!"

Susie and Davy stood ready to go when mom rushed over, "Hold on, you two, I need to get your picture. Smile and say 'cheeseburger!'"

"Cheeseburger!"

Susie laughed as Mom snapped a picture of them. Davy rushed outside and down the porch steps, waiting for Susie on the sidewalk. "Come on already. We're going to be late!"

Susie came off the porch after she gave Mom and Dad a big hug and then caught up with her big brother. Mom was waving to them as they held each other's hand and headed down the sidewalk towards school.

"So, Susie, what do you think of all this first day of school stuff?" asked Davy.

"I don't know. I just want to meet my new teacher. I hope she is pretty like Mommy," she replied.

Davy just shrugged his shoulders as they walked on toward the school. As they were getting closer, Davy began to watch and listen to all the hustle and bustle. The school buses were busy pulling in and out, dropping off students at Thomas Jefferson Elementary School. Students were everywhere.

As Davy and Susie went inside, Davy pointed her in the right direction and asked, "Susie, you remember where to go now, right? It's room 102, okay?"

She smiled at him and said, "Yes, Davy, it is. I remember. I'm not in kindergarten anymore you know, but thanks for reminding me." Davy just smiled back.

After walking his sister to her classroom, Davy walked further down the hall, where he found his classroom, 403. He felt pretty good about going into the 4th grade. Deep down, though, he was a little nervous and was still asking himself the question, *"How will it feel being the new kid in class?"*

The bell finally rang, and all the kids were settling into the classroom. Davy put his lunch bag on the shelf, then grabbed the first open seat he could find. There was chatter in the room as the other kids scurried to find seats of their own. Just then, the door closed with a slight bang, just enough to make Davy jump a tiny bit from his seat. When he turned his head, he spotted his new teacher, Mr. Clark.

Mr. Clark was a tall guy that kind of reminded Davy of Clark Kent. That's superman's name without his cape. His name was Clark, which maybe was what made Davy think of it in the first place, but he seemed like a nice guy.

Tapping his pen on the desk, Mr. Clark said, "Okay, okay, everyone. Quiet down. I'm going to call out your names for attendance. Please answer, "Here" when you hear your name!" Mr. Clark went through the class one by one in alphabetical order. He called out, "Monica Jackson."

"Here!"

"Robert James."

"Here."

"Davy Jones."

"Here."

Then Davy heard a voice come from somewhere behind him in the back of the room. "What is he a pirate or something?" And a couple of little laughs let out.

"Okay, okay, that will be enough of that," Mr. Clark said as he continued with roll call. Davy didn't hear anything after that. He just thought to himself, "*Pirate. Why did he call me a pirate?*" Then it came to him. "*Davy Jones, he was a pirate from the movie, 'Pirates of the Caribbean.' No one ever called me that before.*"

Finally, Davy's focus came back to class as Mr. Clark finished roll call. He said to everyone, "Well, my name is Mr. Clark, in case you haven't figured that out yet from the big letters here on the board that say, "Mr. Clark's 4th grade class." Some more giggles let out. "I want to welcome you all and let you know that I have a great year of learning planned for you. We're going to have some fun together as we go through our studies. I would also like to introduce two new students to our 4th grade class."

As he said that, Davy got a lump in his throat the size of a bullfrog. "First, Ms. Jessica Lambert and second, Mr. Davy Jones." And then came the pirate joke again, "Arrrrmatey... hey, where's your parrot, kid?"

Davy turned to see who was saying these things, and it turns out it was the bigger boy sitting all the way in the back row. Davy didn't know his name, but what he said sure made him feel bad inside, especially since the other kids were laughing as well.

"That will be enough from you, Mr. Solomon," said Mr. Clark. "We're not going to get off to a bad start with you this year, are we?"

"No, Sir, not a problem. Not aaah problem," the boy said with a big grin on his face.

That response didn't sound very convincing to Davy, not even a little. He never had anything like this happen before, and he didn't know what to think. But he did know one thing for sure; he didn't like it. It made him kind of upset inside and hurt his feelings.

Things started to go a little better as Mr. Clark had some of the students help hand out books and some supplies they would need for the schoolwork he had planned for them.

As Davy and his new classmates were gathering their things for the cafeteria, the bell rang for lunch. Davy reached for his lunch bag on the shelf when he felt a little shove from behind him. He wasn't sure what it was or who did it, but it still was a shove. As he turned around, sure enough, it was the big kid from the back row. *"Maybe he was just getting his lunch, too,"* thought Davy. *"No big deal."*

Davy followed the crowd of kids down the hall to the cafeteria and found a seat at one of the empty tables, then two other boys came over and said, "Hey is anyone sitting here?"

"No," Davy replied.

As the boys took a seat, one of them introduced himself, "Hi, my name is Taylor."

The other said, "My name is Jaxson. Where are you from?"

"Well, my family and I just moved here from Smithfield. My dad got a new job."

Taylor said, "Oh yeah, my aunt and uncle live in Smithfield. It's nice there."

"Yeah, I really didn't want to leave, but well, you know, I didn't have much of a choice. But I like our new house. It's nice, and it's right next to the park, pretty much." The three boys finished their lunch just as the bell went off. As they headed back, Jaxson said to Davy, "Hey, don't let Stephen bother you."

"Stephen?"

"Yeah, you know, the kid with the pirate joke."

"Oh, ok," said Davy. "That's Stephen. Nah, that's okay. It was kind of funny, I guess."

Jaxson continued, "Well, he can be mean sometimes, especially to new kids, so don't let him bother you."

"No, I'm all right. He didn't really bother me all that much."

The boys went back to their classroom and got right into the day's work with Mr. Clark. Before long, the bell rang again, letting students know that the first day at Thomas Jefferson Elementary School had officially come to an end.

As they all packed up their things and started heading out of school, Davy looked for Susie just outside of her classroom so they could walk home together. Davy found his little sister, and the two started their way back home.

"Well," Susie said, "How was it?"

Davy looked at her and said, "All right. How about you?"

"It was nice! Miss Abigail is very, very nice, and she's pretty too!"

The two continued their walk, and before long, they were back at their house. Mom was on the front porch, rocking in her chair while waiting for them when she spotted Davy and Susie coming up the steps. "Hey there! So, how was your first day, you two? Tell me all about this new school of yours."

"It was nice, Mommy," Susie shouted. "Miss Abigail is very nice, and she's pretty too Mommy. I really like my new school!"

Davy's answer wasn't quite as enthusiastic as Susie's. He just said, "It was all right, I guess."

"Hmmm." Mom said. "Just all right?"

"Yeah. It was all right," Davy said as he went inside.

Chapter Two

Think it Over

The family showed some examples of love for one another, can you name two examples that you see?

_____

_____

_____

_____

_____

Did Stephen show love or kindness towards Davy on his first day at school?

_____

_____

How could Stephen have shown Davy some love or kindness on his first day of school, instead of being mean to him and hurting his feelings?

_____

_____

_____

_____

_____

Scripture References:

Matthew 22: 37: 39

Jesus replied "Love the Lord God with all your heart and with all your soul and with all your mind. This is the first and greatest commandment. And the second is like it: Love your neighbor as yourself.

1 Corinthians 13: 13

"so now faith, hope, and love abide, these three; but the greatest of these is love

Chapter Three

Dinner Time

Mom called out for dinner. Davy came rushing down the steps from his bedroom in a big swoosh, right over to the kitchen table. Susie followed Davy, making her way to the table, and Dad put his things down from work as he joined them. Mom was putting the last of her delicious-looking food on the table as they all sat down. They all gave thanks for dinner, then took turns in saying their thanks for the good things that God has brought them during the day. Susie wanted to go first.

"God, thank you for my new teacher, Miss Abigail. She is very nice and pretty, like you, Mommy."

"Thank you." Mom smiled at Susie and went next. "God, I'm thankful for you bringing my happy family home safely today."

Dad said, "God, thank you for my day at work, and

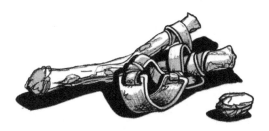

for helping me to complete all my tasks on time with no hang-ups."

It was Davy's turn next, "Ummmmm God, well, I'm not sure. Thank you for the end of the first day of school, I guess."

Mom and Dad just looked at each other, not quite sure what to make of Davy's prayer. So, they listened some more for signs of how Davy was really doing, thinking that maybe Davy didn't have such a good first day at his new school.

"So, Susie, it sounds like you really liked your first day at your new school and your new teacher. You said her name is Miss Abigail, is that right?"

"Yes, Mommy, she is very nice, and she said we are going to have the best time learning new things in her class this year! She said we are going to learn how to count all the way up to 100 and that we will learn to add and subtract. I will even be able to read my own books, Mommy!"

"Wow, that sounds like something to be very excited about; she sounds wonderful, Jelly Bean," Dad said. Jelly Bean was Dad's nickname for Susie. He says it's because he loves jelly beans so much. Then Dad turned and said, "How about your teacher? What is your teacher's name, Davy?"

"His name is Mr. Clark."

"Oh yeah, Mr. Clark. Well, tell me about him. What did you think of your first day in Mr. Clark's class?"

Davy didn't give much of an answer. So Dad said, "You seem a little quiet tonight is everything okay?"

"Yeah, I guess I was just thinking of Jimmy and Cooper, that's all."

"Jimmy and Cooper, huh," said Dad. "Maybe you can try giving them a call later to see how they're doing, what do you think?"

"Yeah, maybe I can see how they're doing." Davy couldn't get the day off his mind. The pirate thing had him thinking about what happened that morning and wondering what might happen next. He hoped the situation with Stephen would just go away. He wanted to make some new friends like his two buddies, Jimmy and Cooper. They would hang out, laugh, and play, and there wouldn't be any mean pirate jokes.

When dinner was over, and the kitchen was cleaned up, the entire family sat down together to relax. Dad said, "Well, Mom, that sure was a good pot roast you made tonight. I'm stuffed!"

"I'm glad you liked it!" she replied. "Davy, did you want to use my phone to give the boys a call to see how their first day of school went, and tell them about your new teacher?"

"All right, Mom." Davy jumped up to get Mom's phone from the table. He found Cooper's number first in the contacts and pushed on his name, Cooper's mom answered the phone.

"Hello, Mrs. Reynolds, can I talk to Cooper, please?"

"Oh, hi, Davy! Just a minute, I call for him. He and Jimmy just went out back to throw the football around, or at least that's what I think they said they were going to do."

"Cooooper! cried out, Mrs. Reynolds. "Davy is on the phone. He would like to talk to you."

Davy could picture Cooper and Jimmy running in, bumping into each other as they came through the door. It was always a race with the two of them.

"Hey Davy, how's it going? Did you start school yet?"

"Yeah, our first day of school was today, like you. Who did you guys get for a teacher this year?"

"We both got Mrs. Ziller," said Cooper. "She's pretty cool. She said we are going to get a pet for our classroom this year. I think it's going to be a turtle or a frog or something like that. How about you? Do you have a frog in your class?"

Davy laughed, listening to his friend. "No, not exactly. More like a toad."

"A toad, really?"

"No, I'm just kidding." Davy started to feel like it wasn't nice to think of Stephen as a toad, but he did let out a little bit of a chuckle thinking about it.

The three boys talked back and forth on the phone for a while. Davy never mentioned to his friends what happened with the pirate joke because he wasn't sure what to do about it just yet. He thought, *"Maybe I shouldn't say anything at all."* He had concerns that if he said anything, the other kids might think he was a tattletale, and it might get even worse than what it already was. *"Maybe I'll just see what happens."*

By the time he got off the phone, it was starting to get late. He had to get ready for bed, so he cleaned up, put on his PJ's, and settled into bed. Mom and Dad had already

tucked Susie in after reading her storybook, and it was Davy's turn next.

"So, Davy, are you feeling a little better now that you got to talk to your friends tonight?" Mom asked.

"Yeah, I'm okay."

"Remember, we are both here for you, Davy, and God is always with you. If you need to, ask him for help, he will always be at your side to guide you along."

"Thanks, Mom, I know."

They each kissed Davy on the head and said, "goodnight." *"Hear that God? I'm going to need your help on this one, okay?"* Davy finished up his prayers and fell asleep.

Chapter Three

Think it Over

The family often gives thanks to God in the story. What can you find in your life to give God thanks for?

_____

_____

_____

_____

_____

Are there people or things in your life that you can say you feel grateful for? List 3

_____

_____

_____

_____

Scripture References:

1 Thessalonians 5:18

Give thanks in all circumstances; for this is God's will for you in Christ Jesus.

Psalm 106:1

Praise the Lord. Give thanks to the Lord for he is good; his love endures forever

Davy seemed to be confused about how to handle things at school. What do you think you would have done if you were Davy?

_____

_____

_____

_____

_____

It is important to report bullying. There is a difference between tattling on someone and telling someone like a teacher or parent about something that is going on that you believe is wrong or hurtful.

- **Tattling is reporting to an adult about someone else's behavior to get them in trouble.**

- **Telling is reporting to a responsible adult about someone else's behavior to help someone – themselves or someone else.**

Give an example of when you might have "tattled" on someone.

_____

_____

_____

_____

_____

How did you feel after tattling?

_____

_____

_____

_____

Have you ever told a responsible adult about something that happened to help someone else?

_____

_____

How did you feel after telling?

_____

_____

_____

_____

_____

<u>Scripture Reference:</u>

Psalm 46: 1

God is our refuge and strength an ever-present help in

trouble.

Chapter Four

Here We Go Again

The alarm rang out in Davy's room. He rubbed his eyes and said out loud, "It's morning already? Boy time sure does go by fast when you're taking a good snooze." So, Davy started his daily routine. Get up, brush teeth, make the bed, get dressed, on and on. Then he thought, *"Oh wait! Maybe Mom made pancakes again!"*

Davy got dressed quickly, gave himself a glance in the mirror to make sure everything was in the right spot, and down the stairs, he ran. He made it to the kitchen to find a bowl of cereal waiting for him. *"Uhhhhh no pancakes, hmm. Oh well, cereal is pretty good too."*

Davy wasn't much of a picky eater; he liked all kinds of stuff. Before he took his first bite, he bowed his head and gave God thanks, and said out loud, "Remember what we talked about God?"

"What was that, Davy?" Mom asked. "I didn't hear you."

"Nothing, Mom, just having my breakfast."

"All right, sweetie, finish up. Your sister is all done and waiting for you."

Davy took the last spoonful of his cereal, slurped down the milk from the bottom of the bowl and wiped his face as he headed for the front door. Susie was sitting on the chair near the door as Davy lifted his backpack to head off to school. Mom came in to wish them a good day, and off they went.

Davy held his little sister's hand as they walked down the sidewalk, and she said to him, "You know Davy, I'm a big girl now. You really don't have to hold my hand anymore, but I kind of like it. It reminds me of Daddy. I love Daddy, don't you, Davy?"

Davy just looked at his little sister, smiled at her, and said, "Yeah, Susie. I do."

As they approached the school, the crowd seemed to get thicker, with all the kids going in the front door. Davy and Susie were just about to go through the door when Davy felt a big push from behind.

"Hey, Pirate. I guess you found your parrot. Look everyone the pirate has his little parrot with him today.

Hey, Parrot. You want a cracker?"

It was Stephen, and this time he was picking on Susie too, Susie didn't know what to say, and Davy was starting to get a little upset. That's his little sister, and he wasn't about to have anyone pick on her.

He turned and said, "Leave us alone." With a loud, shaky voice, he continued, "We aren't bothering you, and she is just a little girl. Go on. Get out of here before I tell on you."

"Ohhh. Are you going to tell on me, Pirate? Who are you going to tell, your mommy?"

Davy just turned away and took Susie by the hand and walked her to her class to make sure she was okay. He asked, "Are you all right?"

"Yeah, but what was that boy talking about parrots and crackers for Davy? What's going on?"

"Don't worry, Susie; I'll take care of it. Everything will be fine. Go into your class now, okay?"

"All right, Davy. I'll see you later."

Davy's cheeks were still red, and he could feel his heart thumping in his chest like a drum. *"What is wrong with this kid?"* He thought, *"Why does he have it out for me like this? I don't even know him, and to talk like that to Susie? She's just a little girl. What am I going to do, God? What am I going to do?"*

Davy went into his classroom, put his things away, and sat in his seat. He looked over his shoulder and could see Stephen in the back of the room pointing his finger at him while telling some other kids what happened. One of the boys made parrot noises, and they all laughed at him. Davy turned around and put his head down for a moment as he gathered himself and settled down. *"I'll work this out; it will be okay. I'll just talk to him and see what's wrong."*

Mr. Clark came in and got the class started. Things moved along okay, and before Davy knew it, the lunch bell rang. Davy grabbed his lunch bag and headed down the hall like he did the day before then took a seat at the first empty table he could find. He started to eat his lunch when guess who shows up? That's right it was Stephen.

Davy turned to look at him when Jaxson and Taylor walked over to the table. "Everything okay here?" Taylor asked.

Davy stood up and asked Stephen, "What's wrong? Why are you so upset with me? I don't even know you."

"Look, kid. You better just watch it! I don't like pirates," he said as he turned and walked away.

"Well, I see Stephen is still at it," Taylor said.

"Yeah," Davy said. "He pushed me coming into school today and made fun of my little sister. I don't get it. He's getting worse, do you guys know why he is acting like this?"

"No, not really," said Jaxson. "That's just the way he's been since he came here last year."

"You mean he just started here in the last year?"

"Yep, but the story about Stephen is he had to stay back a grade at his old school for something. No one knows why, though," added Taylor.

The three boys sat down and had their lunch while talking about other things. For the moment, they forgot what was going on with Stephen. Jaxson asked Davy how he liked everything so far, and Davy had a hard time answering him.

"Well, aside from all the pirate stuff, I kind of like it. Mr. Clark is a good guy, I think it's going to be fun in his class, and the school is nice from what I've seen so far. So yeah, I like it, I guess, but 'you know who' is not making it easy. That's for sure."

"We think you're a nice guy Davy, so if you would like to hang out with us, that will be all right. We can look out for each other, okay?"

"Okay," Davy said. "Thanks. You guys remind me of my two friends from back home. It's nice to meet some guys who aren't mad at me for no reason."

The three new friends laughed a little as they headed back to their classroom. The school day was finishing up without any more problems, and the bell sounded to put day two in the history books. Davy grabbed his things and headed out the door towards Susie's class so he could meet up with her and walk home as usual.

While heading home, they bumped into Jaxson and Taylor, Davy's new friends. "This is my little sister, Susie."

"Hi, nice to meet you. My name is Taylor, and his name is Jaxson. Your brother's a nice guy. We're going to be buddies now, so I guess we'll see you around Susie. Have a good day, you two." And they headed out in the opposite direction.

As they walked home, Susie asked, "What was that all about this morning? That kid was big and mean. I don't like mean people."

"Don't worry, Susie; I'm working it out. He won't bother you anymore."

"I'm going to tell Mommy what happened this morning, and you should tell her that big boy pushed you in the back for no reason at all. That's what you should do, Davy!"

"Susie, Susie, relax. I know, and like I said, I'll figure it out, okay? I promise."

Chapter Four

Think it Over

Stephen continues to bully and give Davy a hard time, and now he is even bullying Susie by calling her names. Bullying can be very difficult; we see Davy tell Stephen to stop! Do you think this was a good idea?

_____

_____

Why?

_____

_____

_____

_____

_____

How would you have handled the situation?

_____

_____

_____

_____

_____

Tell the bully to stop. Again, bullies often do not expect someone to stand up to them. In fact, they often target kids who they believe they can intimidate. As a result, telling a bully to stop in a strong and confident voice can be very effective.

Bullies often count on finding a victim who will not say anything at all. But if you make sure the bully knows he cannot walk all over you, the bully is more likely to stop what he is doing.

Are you courageous enough to stand up to someone who is bullying you or a friend?

_____

_____

Do you believe God is always with you?

_____

_____

Is there something you can share about Him being with you in a time of trouble?

_____

_____

_____

_____

Scripture References:

Luke 17: 3

"If your brother or sister sins against you, rebuke them and if they repent, forgive them.

Joshua 1:9

"Have I not commanded you? Be strong and courageous. Do not be afraid; do not be discouraged, for the LORD your God will be with you wherever you go."

Chapter Five

The Little Parrot Has Something to Say

Davy and Susie had gotten in the door and settled down for a little bit before it was time for dinner. Davy was coming down the steps when Mom had just sounded off the dinner announcement. "Dinner time!"

So everyone headed to the dinner table. As Dad, Davy, and Susie got seated, Mom was setting all the yummy food she prepared on the table, Susie spoke right up about their morning walk to school. "Mommy and Daddy, I want you to know something. Today when Davy and I were going into school, this big mean boy came up behind Davy and gave him a big push in the back! Then he called me a parrot and asked me if I wanted a cracker. I didn't know what he was talking about since I already had my cereal. Why would I want a cracker? I still don't even know what he was talking about, Mommy."

"Davy," Mom said, "What's this all about? Why would this boy push you in the back and say these things?" "I don't know Mom; I don't know. I'm trying to figure that out. It all started yesterday during our roll call for attendance when Mr. Clark called my name. This boy, his name is Stephen, called me a pirate. I guess because Davy Jones is the name of a pirate in a movie. Some of the other kids laughed when he said it, so he's kept it up since then. And this morning, when he saw Susie and me going into school, he called her a parrot and asked if she wanted a cracker. Do you get it? Parrot, do you want a cracker?"

"Yes, Davy, I get it. You know this is not acceptable behavior, and we are going to need to do something about it. We'll have to bring this to your teacher and the school's attention. Davy, we can't allow this behavior to continue. We have to see what's going on with this boy and why he's acting this way."

"Mom, I don't want the other kids to think that I'm a tattletale."

"Is that what you're worried about Davy, what the other kids may think? What if this boy were to hurt someone Davy, would others thinking you're a tattletale matter then?"

Dad asked, "Davy is this why you were so quiet yesterday after school?"

"I guess so, Dad. I didn't know what to do, and I just wanted it to go away. I'd really like things to be more like they were when I was hanging out with Jimmy and Cooper."

"I can understand that you want it to go away, Davy, but this isn't something to take care of on your own. I want you to understand it's okay to get help from your parents or your teacher when it comes to things like this. Davy, bullying is a very serious situation, okay? Please always remember to ask for help with things that aren't clear to you. God trusted us to be your mom and dad here on earth so that we can share the wisdom He has given us to share with you and your sister. Do you understand?"

"Yes, Dad."

"So, here's what we're going to do. We will call the school tomorrow and discuss it with the principal and your teacher. We will get to the bottom of this, so no one gets hurt or upset in any way over this."

"Dad, is Stephen going to get in trouble?"

"I don't know Davy, maybe. You know, when someone makes bad choices, there are consequences that come along with those choices and behaviors. For now, let's wait and see what the school administrators think should be done. Maybe before you go to sleep tonight, you can pray for Stephen. Pray that he can learn from all of this and will turn away from bullying and pushing other kids around."

They all finished their dinner and moved on from their talk. After helping Mom to clear the table and wash the dishes, the family moved to the living room to watch some television. Before long, it was time for bed. Davy got himself all ready, jumped into bed, and pulled the covers up nice and tight around him. Mom and Dad came in to kiss him and say goodnight. They told him that everything would be all right and to get his rest. Davy thanked his mom and dad and said, "Goodnight. I love you guys. You're the best parents ever."

Mom and Dad left Davy's room. As they did, Davy was saying his prayers. He thanked God for all the things he was grateful for, but tonight he also asked God to look at Stephen's heart. He asked God to help him with whatever may be bothering him, so he would not be so angry, and he wouldn't want to hurt other kids anymore. Davy also asked God to open Stephen's heart that perhaps he and Davy may even become friends one day.

After saying his prayers and knowing his mom and dad were going to help with the situation, and that God loves him, Davy drifted off to a peaceful sleep.

Chapter Five

Think it Over

Susie and the family sit down for dinner, and Susie speaks right up as she often does and reports the morning bullying to her mom and dad. Was she right for doing this?

_____

_____

Why?

_____

_____

_____

_____

_____

Report the bullying to an adult. The best way to prevent bullying is to report it. Without adult intervention, bullying will often continue or escalate.

Scripture Reference:

Proverbs 22: 6

Start children off on the way they should go, and even when they are old, they will not turn from it.

That evening Davy prays for Stephen so that whatever is bothering him may come out, and he can get over whatever is upsetting him and causing him to act badly toward others.

Do you think that God wants us to pray for people like Stephen?

_____

_____

Why?

_____

_____

_____

_____

_____

Why should we pray for people who hurt us? Kids bully for many reasons. Some bully because they feel insecure. Picking on someone who seems

emotionally or physically weaker can create a feeling of being more important, popular, or in control. In other cases, kids bully because they simply don't know that it's unacceptable to pick on kids who are different because of size, looks, race, or religion.

Scripture References:

Luke 23:34

Jesus said, "Father forgive them, for they do not know what they are doing," And they divided up his clothes by casting lots.

Matthew 5:44

"But I tell you to love your enemies and pray for anyone who mistreats you."

Chapter Six

As They Say, Third Times A Charm

The alarm clock rang out once again in Davy's room. Like the two days before, Davy woke up, rubbed his eyes, and jumped out of bed.

"Here we go. It's day three of school. I wonder what's going to happen today? I almost wish I had a stomach ache or a fever, something that would keep me out of school. I just don't want to see Stephen. Especially once Mom and Dad call the school, that may just make him even madder if he gets in trouble because of me."

Davy knew better. He knew that sometimes we need to do things that aren't very exciting, and we may not want to do them at all. Our days aren't always perfect, and Davy also knew that something good might come out of all this. That's what he hoped for and knew he needed to think about most.

So, Davy got himself ready and headed for the kitchen. There was Susie, sitting at the table having her blueberry muffin.

"Hey, Davy," Susie said, "Are you going to have a blueberry muffin? They're really good. Mom made them and put extra berries in just for us. They're really, really good!"

"Good morning," Mom said. "How are we this morning?"

"Ehhh," Davy replied. "Alright, I guess."

Mom had a feeling Davy was troubled, and she certainly knew why. "Don't worry, Davy, everything will get straightened out and will be fine. Just wait. Your Dad and I will see to it, I promise. We'll work with the school and your teacher to get to the bottom of this."

"Okay, I guess." Davy started eating his blueberry muffin. He said a quiet prayer asking God to make the day go by without any troubles. He thanked Him for all the goodness He brings to his family and for helping him learn how to handle the harder days—to be happy no matter what. As he finished his muffin, he thought that Susie was right. *"Mom's muffins are really good."*

He cleaned up, grabbed his things, then called out to Susie, "Hey Susie, where are you? It's time to go!"

"Here I am! Let's go, Davy. I'm ready."

She grabbed her lunch bag as they headed out the door, waving to Mom as they left for school. Susie took her brother's hand, and they walked down the sidewalk. As they got a little closer, Susie said, "I'm scared, Davy. What if that boy does something again today?"

"Well, we'll see. Don't be scared."

They got nearer to school, Taylor and Jaxson joined up with them. That brought a little relief to Davy. He started to think that Stephen wouldn't bother them now that they had him outnumbered. Davy felt a little better as they went into school. He stopped to see Susie to her classroom and headed for his own.

He put his things away like he had the last two days and sat at his desk. Davy turned to see if Stephen was at his desk yet, but he wasn't there. Davy felt better thinking, *"Maybe he won't be here today, and I won't have to worry about him bothering me."* But Davy thought a little more and realized that wasn't the answer. He knew he needed to face this straight on and get it fixed because it wasn't just him who Stephen was picking on. It was his little sister too, and maybe even other kids he didn't know.

Davy looked around and noticed that the class was pretty filled up, but Stephen and Mr. Clark were not in the room yet. His belly started to feel a little squirmy once again. Just a moment later, the door opened. Mr. Clark and Stephen both came in together.

"Hmmm. What is this?" He thought. *"Did something happen already?"* Stephen walked right past Davy's desk and gave him a serious look. Davy thought, *"Yep, something happened all right. That look on his face says something happened for sure, but I wonder what?"*

"Okay, class, attention up front, please," said Mr. Clark. "Take out your history books and turn to page 10. Did we all remember to read our first chapter on the….."

Davy's mind wandered away for a moment, thinking of what might have happened between Stephen and Mr. Clark. That look on Stephen's face. What did it mean for Davy? Was Stephen going to be even madder if he got called into the principal's office because Davy said something about the first couple days of school?

Davy's attention came back to the sound of Mr. Clark's voice as he asked about the inventions of Benjamin Franklin and his discovery of electricity. The conversation went on, and the morning seemed to go by rather fast. The lesson finished up just before the lunch bell rang. Davy began to look around the hall for Taylor and Jaxson to see if they had come out of class yet.

"Hey Davy," said a voice from behind. It was Taylor. "Are you ready for lunch?" Jaxson followed right behind, and the three boys went to the cafeteria together, took a seat, then started talking about their after-school plans.

"Davy, you'll have to see if you can come over to my house one of these days. I don't live too far from here, just over on Farr St. It's called Farr St. but it's really not that far from here." The boys laughed a little bit as they enjoyed their lunch.

Davy turned around to see Stephen standing right behind him. "Hey Pirate, thanks for telling on me. Maybe I should call you tattletale instead. What do you think?"

"We think you should call him Davy since that's his name," Jaxson said. "Thanks to you, my parents have to come to school tomorrow to sit with Mr. Clark and Mr. Cartwright, and now I'm probably going to get in trouble because of you!"

"Because of me?" Davy said. "What did I do? You're the one who wouldn't stop with the name-calling and pushing. I asked you to stop. I also told you I was going to tell someone if you didn't, but you didn't listen."

"I better not get in any trouble, that's all I can say," said Stephen as he walked away from the table.

"Boy, can you believe that guy?" Taylor said. "I don't understand why he's acting like that. He just doesn't get it."

"It's not that hard to be kind to people," Jaxson said. "He's a real grumpy kid, that one."

The boys finished their lunch and headed back to their classroom. Davy took his seat and looked over his shoulder to see what was going on behind him. Stephen just gave him this look that would stop a bear in his tracks and send him climbing up a tree, but Davy wasn't scared of him anymore. He was more curious as to why he was acting the way he was. It just didn't seem right to him, so he wondered why. *"What's behind this?"* He thought.

Mr. Clark came in, and the class got back to work. Math first, then some reading, and before you knew it the bell was ringing again. Day number three had finished up. The kids all grabbed their belongings and headed out the door. Mr. Clark called out to Davy, "Can I talk to you for a moment please?"

Davy turned and said, "Sure, Mr. Clark."

"Davy, I'm sorry to hear you were having a hard time with Stephen. Your parents called the school this morning and informed us of the situation. I want you to know that we are looking into it and are going to take action to get things fixed. I do not approve of bullying in any way and will not allow that behavior in my class or this school. We have already called Stephen's parents and made an appointment for them to come in right away to address the situation. Stephen had a few issues last year that we thought had resolved, but I guess they're back again. So, we'll see what's going on. Davy, I want you to know you did the right thing telling your parents about this. There is no shame in getting the proper help with things before they get out of hand or someone gets hurt."

"My sister is the one who brought it up with my parents. I didn't know what to do."

"Getting adults involved in this case was the right thing to do," added Mr. Clark. "Never hesitate to talk to your parents or me when you're not sure about something bigger than you. And I don't mean bigger as in size. I mean bigger than your life experiences. Some things can be confusing. That's why it helps to have wise people around you like your mom and dad or your grandparents. It's always good to confide in someone who really cares about you and will help you make good decisions. It will also help you grow in wisdom, so you can make good decisions on things as you grow up."

"I guess so," Davy said. "I didn't want to have any trouble being the new kid in class, and I want to make new friends here. That's all."

"That's certainly understandable, Davy, and we want you to feel welcome here at Thomas Jefferson Elementary school as well. Let's get this straightened out so we can all have a good year learning and making friends, okay Davy?"

"Yes, Sir. That sounds good to me!"

As Davy and Susie headed home after school, Susie asked, "Did you hear anything from that boy today Davy?"

"Yeah, Susie, he was called into the principal's office and wasn't too happy about it. That's for sure."

"What did he do?"

"He didn't really do anything, but he did say his mom and dad have to go into school and sit down with Mr. Cartwright and Mr. Clark."

"Ewww, he's going to get in trouble now," she said.

"We'll see. Maybe he'll just apologize, and we can forget the whole thing."

"Do think he should apologize to me, Davy?"

"Yes, Susie. He wasn't very nice to you; he hurt your feelings and scared you, didn't he?"

"Yes, that was scary when he pushed you. I didn't know what to do. If he apologizes to me, Davy, I will forgive him. Daddy says it's good to forgive people, right? Maybe he didn't know what he was doing was so scary for a little girl."

The two were soon at the door of their house and went inside, unpacked their things and settled in a bit. Mom came into the room, welcomed them home, and asked, "How was school today?"

"I don't know, Mom. Stephen was pretty upset about going to the principal's office. He said at lunch that he better not get in trouble because I told on him. His mom and dad have to go in and talk with Mr. Cartwright and Mr. Clark tomorrow."

"Yes, I heard that part from the office secretary. Your Dad and I are going into school tomorrow afternoon to discuss what happens next."

"I hope Stephen's parents talk to him about his behavior, that he understands what he's doing is wrong, and he just agrees to stop."

"Yes, Davy, that's what we are all thinking we would like to have happen here. So, why don't you say a prayer for him tonight, okay? Just believe that this will all work out well for everyone."

Chapter Six

Think it Over

Davy's friends are beginning to show support for their new friend.

Do you think it is important to have friends to help stand against bullies or maybe be a friend to someone who is being bullied?

_____

_____

Why?

_____

_____

_____

_____

_____

Do you know what it means to be a good friend?

_____

_____

What are some things you can do to assure someone that you are their good friend?

_____

_____

_____

_____

_____

Scripture Reference:
Philippians 2:4

"Let each of you look not only to his own interest, but also to the interest of others."

Davy and Susie discuss forgiveness; do you believe forgiveness is important?

_____

_____

Why?

_____

_____

_____

_____

_____

Scripture Reference:

Matthew 6: 14-15

"For if you forgive other people when they sin against you, your heavenly Father will also forgive you. But if you do not forgive others their sins, your Father will not forgive your sins.

Chapter Seven

Hi, Ho Hi, Ho; It's Off To School We Go

The morning was here. As Susie was heading to the kitchen for breakfast, she was whistling and singing a song, "Hi, Ho Hi, Ho; it's off to school we go, we'll learn some stuff and Hmmm Hmmm Hmmm ... it's off to school we go! Deee dee de dee...."

"Boy, you're in a good mood today," said Mom.

"Yeah, Mommy, I like that song the Seven Dwarfs sing in the Snow White movie. It might be my favorite. Hmmm. Well, I don't know. Maybe Cinderella is my favorite. I don't know; I kind of like them all, Mommy."

Mom just looked at Susie and chuckled, "Oh Susie, you're such a little cutie pie. I love you to the moon and back!"

"Hahahaha. I love you too, Mommy!"

Davy came down and joined them at the breakfast table. "Good morning, Mr. Davy. How did you sleep last night?"

"I slept pretty well, Mom. I'm hungry. What's for breakfast?"

"I thought today you could have some scrambled eggs and toast. What do you think?"

"Yeah, that sounds good. I haven't had that in a while. Bring on the eggs!"

"Cock-a-doodle-do, I'll have some too!" Susie said.

Mom started to laugh. "You're awfully silly this morning Susie. Silly, silly, silly."

The kids were laughing at the table as they waited for their breakfast. Mom didn't want to bring up the school day since Davy seemed so relaxed, so she just gave them their eggs and toast while they enjoyed their laugh. Davy said a prayer before he ate his breakfast, giving thanks as he normally does.

"Here we go, God. Is today the day I'll find out if Stephen is going to be nice, or is he going to try to punch me in the nose? I sure hope he is going to settle down and be nice. God, it's so much better to be nice than it is to be angry and mean, right? So please, God, whatever you need to do, please

help me get through this at school, and may everyone be safe."

Davy and Susie finished up their breakfast, cleaned up, then grabbed their things to head off to school. They marched off the porch together, heading towards Thomas Jefferson Elementary, hand in hand, side by side. Just about the same spot as the day before, Taylor and Jaxson showed up.

"Hey, Susie! Hey, Davy!" The boys called out, "How are you doing today?"

"Hi guys, how are you doing? Are you ready for the end of our first week of school?"

"Yeah, I know I could use a break," said Jaxson.

"I need some playtime," said Taylor.

"Yeah, I'm with you!" Davy said, "Maybe you guys can come over to my house so we can go to the park I was telling you about. The slide is giant size and as fast as lightning!"

"That sounds like a good idea, Davy," added Susie. "If you like going around in circles really fast, there's a nice merry-go-round there. It's my favorite! I like the swings too, but the merry-go-round is still my favorite."

"I can talk to my mom later and find out," Davy said. "After school, let's trade phone numbers, okay? This way, we can get permission, and I can give you my address and stuff."

"Sounds like a great idea. I really like giant slides," said Taylor. The kids laughed a little bit, then they all went into the school together.

"See you later," Jaxson said to Susie.

"Yeah, see you later, Susie," Davy said, as he waved to his little sister.

Hanging around with his new friends took Davy's mind off Stephen and that whole mess. As the kids settled into Mr. Clark's class, they noticed Ms. Tompkins, the student aid, was in his chair. She usually helps out in both fourth-grade classes when they need a little extra teacher power between the two rooms. This morning was the first time Davy had met her.

"Hello everyone, my name is Ms. Tompkins. I'm filling in for Mr. Clark this morning. He is tied up in a meeting and will be a little late, so he asked me to get things started. Let's open our history books to page twenty-three, please. Who can tell me who invented the radio?"

Davy's thoughts began to shift from the radio to what was going on in the principal's office with Stephen and what was going to happen when he came back into the room. Gathering his thoughts, Davy refocused his attention on what Ms. Tompkins was discussing with the class. They were studying inventions. Davy had read the chapter, but his thoughts were still wandering back and forth. He knew he had to pay attention to what they were learning, but it seemed hard at the time because it was difficult to keep his mind off what might be happening at the meeting just down the hall in the principal's office.

"Davy, can you tell me who invented the light bulb?"

Davy answered back, "Thomas Edison, Ms. Tompkins."

"Very good, Davy." The study went on; Davy got back to keeping his mind on what was being taught, and not so much on the principal's office.

Not too long after class had started, Mr. Clark came into the room, but he was by himself. No Stephen. *"I wonder what could have happened?"* Davy was thinking, *"Where is he? Why is he not in class? Did they kick him out of school?"* His mind was racing with different thoughts as to what could have happened this morning, knowing he had a part in it.

Mr. Clark got himself situated while Ms. Tompkins stayed a little longer in the classroom as we shifted things over to English. Davy got his book out and followed along, keeping his attention on his schoolwork. He figured that worrying about the situation with Stephen wasn't going to help him at all, so it wasn't worth his being distracted. He thought, *"God, you're there, right? It's going to be okay, isn't it?"*

Davy zeroed back in on what was happening in the classroom, and before he knew it, the bell was sounding off for lunch. Davy jumped up, grabbed his lunch, and headed out the door. He turned to see where Taylor and Jaxson were. He spotted them, and they all headed down the hall together and sat at a table.

Davy couldn't help himself. He said, "Did you guys notice that Stephen isn't in class today?"

"He's not?" Taylor said.

"No, he's not. That's because he had to go to the principal's office, remember? And his parents had to go with him. I hope he didn't get kicked out of school because of me," Davy said.

"They can kick you out of school for being a bully?"

"I think so," Davy said. "I'm not sure, but I think so. My dad said Stephen could get in big trouble for this. Boy, I really wish he wasn't acting like that. I don't want to get anyone in trouble."

Jaxson said, "But Davy, remember you didn't make him do anything, he chose to push you and call you and Susie names! It was wrong for him to do that. He should never pick on someone just because they're new in our school. Really, he shouldn't pick on anyone for anything, right? So, relax. Whatever happens to him now is because of what he did, not what you did. You asked him to stop, but he didn't."

"I know, but I feel a little bad for him for some reason," Davy said. The boys moved the conversation from Stephen to talk about what they might do at the park. They had a couple of laughs and finished their lunch just before the bell went off to head back into class.

Finally, the day was over, and it was time to head home for the weekend. As the kids went out the door, Mr. Clark asked Davy to come over and talk with him at his desk.

"What is it, Mr. Clark?"

"Davy, as you know, we had a meeting with Stephen and his parents today. You also know that your parents were coming in to visit us as well. I want to tell you that things went very well at that meeting this morning and I believe you're going to see some big changes in our friend, Stephen, moving forward. I just wanted you to know that, all right? Now, I'm going to leave the finer details for your

parents to explain to you when you get home. Okay, young man? As I said, we want all of our students here to feel welcome and safe when they come to school. You enjoy your weekend, and I'll see you first thing Monday morning."

"Yes, Sir," Davy answered. "And you have a good weekend, too, Sir." Davy turned and left the room. When he went out to the hall, he found Taylor, Jaxson, and Susie waiting for him.

"Everything okay, Davy?" Susie asked.

"Yeah, Susie, everything is okay. Let's get home all right?"

The four headed for the door. It was a nice, sunny afternoon, and it got the kids thinking about playing outside. "Hey, let's trade phone numbers so we can make plans to go to the park," suggested Jaxson. They each wrote their numbers on a piece of paper and headed home.

Susie asked Davy again, "Is everything all right, Davy?"

"Yeah, Susie, like I said before, it's all right."

"Well, why did you have to stay in Mr. Clark's class after the bell rang?"

"He just needed to tell me something, that's all. Everything is okay."

The two quickly found themselves at the front porch and went inside. Davy's mom and dad were both there waiting for them to come in.

"Hey, guys! How's it going today? Did you have a nice day at school?" Dad asked.

Susie, of course, spoke up first. "Yes, Daddy. I had a wonderful day at school. Today I got to do finger painting during art, and I made a picture of a puppy chewing a bone."

"Really, Susie, a puppy chewing a bone? Hmmm. Well, that's interesting."

"Yeah, and you want to know why Daddy?"

"Sure, Jelly Bean. I would love to know why."

"Because I would like to get a puppy for Christmas this year, that's why. And I already have a name picked out for him. His name will be Rusty."

"Well, well. You already have a name, do you? We'll have to see what we can do about that and if Santa Claus even has any puppies at the North Pole named Rusty. Hmmm. Rusty. How about that?" Dad said as he was scratching his head.

"Davy," Mom asked, "how about you? Did you do any finger painting today?"

"No, Mom, we don't do finger painting in fourth grade."

"Oh, really, okay. You know finger painting is fun no matter what grade you're in. We went to your school today. Would you like to sit down and talk about what happened?"

"Yeah, Mom, I've been waiting all day. You know Stephen wasn't even in class, then at the end of the day, Mr. Clark told me that things went well. He said you would fill me in on the details."

"All right, let's have a seat and talk this over. It's our understanding that when Mr. and Mrs. Solomon went into school with Stephen, they were very upset to hear that their boy was behaving the way he was. They felt very bad about it and apologized to the principal for his behavior. Then they told Mr. Cartwright that Stephen has been carrying some anger around with him from when he was at his former school."

"You see Davy, Stephen was bullied at his old school, and the bullying was so bad, Stephen wouldn't even go to school. He missed so much time that he had to repeat the second grade. Stephen was too afraid to tell his parents what was happening, so he wasn't honest with them. He just kept telling them he wasn't feeling well. After so many trips to the doctor's office and not finding anything wrong, he finally told them the truth. There was a group of children who were making fun of his red hair and calling him names just because he has freckles. He was feeling so badly about his freckles and red hair that he just wanted to stay away from school and those children saying those horrible things to him."

"But Mom, you taught us that God made us perfect just the way we are, doesn't Stephen know that?"

"I don't know Davy, maybe not."

"What is going to happen to Stephen? Is he coming back to school?"

"Yes, Davy, they had given him a warning and some advice for his parents on where to get some help. As long as he stops bullying, he will be allowed back in school. The school will be watching his behavior for any problems like this going forward. Hopefully, Stephen gets the help he needs to get over what happened to him, and he corrects his actions in the future."

"I feel bad that Stephen was getting picked on. It must have been awful to have someone make fun of the way he looks."

"I'm sure it was Davy, but maybe now Stephen will work through that and start to feel better about things and learn not to act badly toward others."

"I hope so, Mom, that would be a good thing for him. I wonder if there is anything I can do that might help him."

"I'm not sure, Davy. Why don't you give it some thought, pray a bit, then see what comes to mind?"

After Davy talked with his mom and dad, and the family had spent some time watching TV after dinner, he went to get settled in for bed. As he laid his head down on his big fluffy pillow, he began saying his prayers. Davy was sure to make a special request that God would give him some direction on what he should do next at school with Stephen and how they can overcome what happened and what to do to move forward in this situation at school.

Chapter Seven

Think it Over

Davy shows us that he really relies on God to direct his day, and he does this by praying to God and having heartfelt conversation.

Do you think this can help you in your day?

_____

_____

How?

_____

_____

_____

_____

_____

Why do you think prayer is important?

_____

_____

_____

_____

_____

Scripture Reference:

James 1:5

"If any of you lacks wisdom, let him ask God, who gives generously to all without reproach, and it will be given him."

Mr. Clark plays a big role in the intervention process and understands that bullying is a serious issue. If you or someone you know is being bullied at school, it is important to address the situation with the school teacher and administrators so that the situation can be resolved quickly and with as little damage as possible.

Scripture Reference:

Romans 15: 5

"Now, the God of patience and consolation grant you to be like-minded one toward another according to Christ Jesus."

Davy showed a tremendous amount of understanding for Stephen when he learned Stephen was bullied at his past school and is even willing to help Stephen.

How do you see Davy's actions towards the person who was picking on him?

_____

_____

_____

_____

_____

Empathy is the ability to understand and share the feelings of another.

Can you give an example of a time when you felt empathy for someone?

_____

_____

_____

_____

_____

<u>**Scripture Reference:**</u>

2 Corinthians 1 3:4

"Blessed be the God and Father of our Lord Jesus Christ, the Father of mercies and God of all comfort, who comforts us in all our affliction, so that we may be able to comfort those who are in any affliction, with the comfort with which we ourselves are comforted by God."

Chapter Eight

Let The Sun Shine In

The morning sun shone brightly. The rays seemed to peek through Davy's window just enough to get his attention. As he was waking up, he realized it was Saturday and remembered that Taylor and Jaxson were coming over to go to the park.

With great excitement, Davy jumped up out of bed, splashed some water on his face, and headed to the kitchen. Mom was already there when he came in.

"Good morning, sleepyhead! How are you this beautiful Saturday morning?"

"Good morning, Mom. I'm good. What time is it?"

"It's almost 9:30. You slept in late this morning. You must have been pretty tired."

"I guess. Yeah, I guess so." Davy said while rubbing

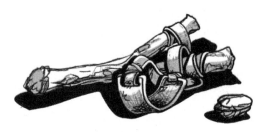

his eyes again.

"Well, how about a nice breakfast to get you started? You'll need some energy for all the playing you boys have planned for today."

"Sounds good to me. What are we having?"

"I made some waffles for Dad and your sister. I can whip up some more for you."

"Sure, waffles sound good to me. Do we have any strawberries to put on top?"

"As a matter of fact, yes, we do!"

"That's what I'll have then. Waffles with strawberries on top, please." Mmmmm, breakfast couldn't get to the table fast enough for Davy. He really likes waffles, not quite as much as banana pancakes, but they're very close to the top of his list of favorites.

The smell of the waffles cooking was a pleasant smell for Davy, and he couldn't wait to dig in. When they were ready, Mom brought them to the table and put them down in front of Davy.

"Oh boy, Mom. These look really good!"

"Thanks!" Mom replied.

Davy said his prayers, thanking God for his family, the things that God has given them, and of course, those scrumptious waffles his mom made. When he finished his breakfast, he went back to his room to get ready for the weekend of playing and having fun he had planned with his new friends. After he was ready and had completed his chores, Davy went downstairs to wait for his friends to get there.

It wasn't too long before Taylor's mom arrived to drop him and Jaxson off for the afternoon. The three boys were all kinds of excited to go to the park and play on the rides. Jaxson brought a frisbee and his football with him. These friends were ready to play!

Taylor's mom came up onto the porch to say hello to Davy's mom. It was the first time Taylor and Jaxson were at Davy's, so their moms wanted to take a few minutes over coffee to get to know one another. As they chatted, the boys immediately began to throw the football around the front yard and play some form of touch football that only they could make up. They were laughing and making up the rules up as they played.

Davy's mind couldn't have been further away from the things that had been happening at school this past week. His spirit soared high as he enjoyed playing and being free of those concerns for the moment. It was

Saturday, he had some new friends and was just living life, being happy as a young boy should.

Their moms finished up their coffee and agreed to a time for a pick-up from their first get together.

"Okay, boys, you can head off to the park. Davy, your dad and I will be there in just a minute. You know the rules. Please share them with Taylor and Jaxson, and we will see you in a bit."

Taylor's mom said goodbye and told the boys to follow the rules that Mr. and Mrs. Jones have and to be on their best behavior.

"Okay, Mom," shouted Taylor.

"Thanks! I love you. See you later," said Taylor's mom as she got in her car.

The three ran down the sidewalk toward the park. They were racing to see who would make it to the slide first. They were having the best time, and things were just getting started. *The sun is shining, it's an absolutely perfect day*," Davy thought, as he remembered days of playing with Jimmy and Cooper.

"There it is, you guys, the slide."

This slide stood as high as the trees and shined in the sun with beauty that only a child could understand. They stood at the bottom of the slide ladder, looking up.

Step-by-step, and one by one they climbed to the top and made their way down the slide, letting out screams of pure excitement as they swooshed to the bottom.

"Wow!!" Jaxson let out.

Then came Taylor, "Woo-hoo!!!"

And finally, Davy, speeding to the ground.
"AAHAAAA!! What did I tell you? Is that fast or what?"

"Wow, Davy, that was so cool. Let's do it again."
From top to bottom, they went time after time, just having a great time together.

Davy's mom and dad showed up at the park with Susie, and called out to the boys, "What do you think? Is it fast enough for you?"

"Yes, Mrs. Jones, this is awesome!"

After a dozen or so rides down the slide, the boys went to the swings. They lined up and challenged each other to see who could go the highest. They pumped their legs as fast and as hard as they could, back and forth. They laughed as the swings carried them to the sky and down again. A real bond of friendship was starting to take root. The boys were becoming the best of friends, being there for one another, helping each other, walking their journey together.

With so much exercise from all their playing and running around, they needed a time out. Thankfully Davy's Mom had packed a snack.

"How about water? Would anyone like some?" asked Davy's mom. "You look like you can use it after all that running around. I packed some apple slices and grapes, so help yourself!"

The boys dug into the bowl of fruit as if they hadn't eaten in a week. They found out that it takes a lot of energy to ride that slide, and the day wasn't even halfway through yet. So, after a quick snack, the boys were back at play. "Let's throw the Frisbee around," Taylor suggested. And off they went.

Time seemed to stand still for them. It was a wonderful day of playing and friendship, but like all things, there is an ending point. As the sun began to set a bit in the sky, Davy's dad said, "Well, boys, I hope you had a good time! It's just about time to head back home for dinner. Taylor, your mom will be at the house soon to take you guys home."

So, the boys grabbed their things and headed off to Davy's house. As they walked up the road, Jaxson said, "Davy, that was fun. I really had a great time! Thanks for inviting us over to play."

"It was awesome," Taylor added, "it was so awesome!"

The boys sat on the porch waiting for Taylor's mom. They were already making plans for another get-together.

"Maybe you can come over to my house, Davy?" suggested Jaxson. "I have a basketball hoop set up in my driveway. Maybe we can play basketball?"

"Yeah, that sounds like fun! Let's see what my mom says, okay?"

It wasn't long before Taylor's mom pulled in the driveway. "Let's go, boys," she said, sticking her head out the car window. The two boys jumped up, headed to the car and got in. They all waved goodbye as they backed out of the driveway.

"Thanks again Davy, we had a blast!!!"

"See you, guys. Talk to you later!" Davy shouted from the porch.

As they drove off, Davy turned to go inside. "Davy," said Dad. "Your mom and I talked it over, and we've decided to go out for dinner tonight. What if we go to Giuseppe's for a pizza? Yeah?"

"That sounds like a really good idea!! Can we get pepperoni, Dad?"

"We'll see Davy. Let's find out what the girls would like, okay?"

Chapter Eight

Think It Over

The new friends are starting to form a bond of true friendship. Friends are important in our life's journey.

Friendship is an important element in a fulfilled, contented life, and those who have close friends, whether one or two or a multitude, will usually be happy and well adjusted.

Friends can, at times, cause us grief and hardship, but they mostly have a positive influence in our life; friends can console and help us when we are in trouble or in need of support.

Can you think of a time when a friend was there to help you through a tough time?

_____

_____

Give an example of a time you were there to help a friend in need.

_____

_____

_____

_____

_____

The book of Proverbs gives us wisdom for navigating the complexities of our relationships. And more specifically, friendships, even what to look for in a true friend.

<u>Scripture References:</u>

Proverbs 13:20

"He who walks with the wise grows wise, but a companion of fools suffers harms."

Proverbs 27:17

"As iron sharpens iron, so one man sharpens another."

Proverbs 18:24

"One who has unreliable friends soon comes to ruin, but there is a friend who sticks closer than a brother."

Chapter Nine

Jones, Party of Four

Davy and his family happily piled into their minivan and headed to Giuseppe's for the best pizza in all the land. "Davy, you must be hungry after all that running around you and your friends did today."

"Oh boy, am I! I think I can eat a whole pizza by myself today," he laughed.

Susie was concerned, "I want pizza too, Mommy."

Mom smiled and said, "Don't worry, honey, Giuseppe has enough pizza for everyone."

Dad pulled into the parking lot, searching for a spot and one opened up, right in front. "Hey, today is my lucky day! Look at that. Right in front."

They all quickly climbed out and headed for the door of the restaurant. Davy could smell the pizza in the air as soon as he got out of the car. The aroma was all around. He

smacked his lips and said, "Come on, everyone. Let's go!"

They entered the restaurant, and while waiting to be seated, Davy spotted Stephen with his mom and dad, or so Davy figured since he never met his parents before. They were on their way out of Giuseppe's. Feeling a bit awkward, Davy froze, not knowing what to do. As they got closer, the two families crossed paths. Davy had nowhere to go but straight ahead.

Without knowing what else to do, Davy said, "Hello."

Stephen answered back, "Hello, Davy."

For one split-second, Davy thought, *"Hey. He didn't call me Pirate."*

"Davy, I owe you and Susie an apology for the way I was acting towards you. I want to say I'm sorry to you both." He reached out his hand for a handshake as if to signal a truce. Davy just stood there for a second and then extended his hand as well.

He said with a little jitter to his voice, "Thank you, and apology accepted."

Right away, Susie stuck her hand out, saying, "That goes for me too. Apology accepted."

The four parents just looked at one another and smiled. Mrs. Solomon had a tear in her eye as they passed by. They wished each other a nice night and went on their way.

The hostess came over to seat Davy and his family. He followed along without saying anything at first. As they sat at their table, Davy looked up and scratched his head. "That is just what I have been asking God for this whole time. That we can be nice to one another, so this whole thing would just go away."

"Well, Davy, it seems to me that God was listening, and things are on that path now. Who knows? Maybe you and Stephen can even become friends," Dad said.

"Yeah. You never know. Maybe we can," Davy thought.

It wasn't too much longer before two steaming hot pizzas arrived at the Jones' table. One with pepperoni and one with lots of cheese. "Okay, okay," Mom said. "Slow down before you burn your tongue, you two boys are impossible."

"Yeah, impossible!" Susie added.

Dad and Davy just looked at each other and chuckled. As they reached for that pepperoni pizza, Davy said, "What a day."

Dad began to pray. "We have lots to be grateful for today, family. Let's always remember that all good things come to us from above, and all things can be resolved through prayer and faith, which gives us hope for a brighter tomorrow. Amen!"

Susie joyfully said, "Let's have pizza!!" They all laughed out loud and enjoyed their dinner at Giuseppe's that night, growing closer as a family.

Chapter Nine

Think It Over

In this chapter, we see the two boys arrive at an unexpected meeting, one that could have been very uncomfortable for everyone, children and parents alike. But instead, it turns out to be a step in a new direction for the two boys.

God often uses bad or uncomfortable things or situations to bring good or healing to a situation.

How might you have felt if you were Davy?

_____

_____

_____

_____

_____

Now, change things up; think of how you may have felt if you were Stephen.

_____

_____

_____

_____

_____

Scripture Reference:

Ephesians 4:32

"Be kind to one another, tenderhearted, forgiving one another, as God in Christ forgave you."

Stephen has come to an understanding that what he did was wrong and wants to apologize for his actions.

How do you feel when you understand that your action was the wrong thing to do?

_____

_____

_____

_____

_____

Scripture Reference:

1 John 1:9

"If we confess our sins, he is faithful and just to forgive us our sins and to cleanse us from all unrighteousness."

We hear Davy comment on how things worked out just as he had hoped and prayed for, that the two can be nice to one and other. It's a wonderfully spiritual feeling when God answers our prayers.

Can you think of a time when God answered a prayer in your life?

_____

_____

And how did that make you feel?

_____

_____

_____

_____

_____

<u>Scripture Reference:</u>

John 15:7

"If you abide in me, and my words abide in you, ask whatever you wish, and it will be done for you."

Chapter Ten

All Weekends Lead to a Monday Morning

Davy climbed into bed and replayed the weekend in his mind. He was thinking about how much fun it was playing at the park with his new friends. Dinner at Giuseppe's, a picnic at the lake, and singing in his church choir. All those great things are now part of his memories.

When Davy's Mom and Dad came in to say goodnight, Davy reached up and gave them both a big hug. "This was a great weekend," He said. "Thank you. You guys are the best!"

"Well, Davy, we think you're the best too. Sleep well, son. I love you!" Dad said as they turned out the light in Davy's room.

Davy closed his eyes and said, "God, thank you for such a beautiful weekend. God, it was all so perfect! I had a great time, and I didn't forget about Stephen. I need to know what's next. I need to know how to move forward

from here. Can you please walk with me as I go?" It wasn't but a moment after he finished praying, it seemed as if he heard, "I sure will son." He closed his eyes and fell asleep with a smile on his face.

Several hours later, the alarm clock sounded in Davy's room. *"Boy, it's morning already?"* He thought, *"Here we go."* Davy did his daily thing and kept himself on time, moving through the routine. He peeked in the mirror to see how he did. This morning he gave himself a wink of approval before he headed down the steps for breakfast.

Susie was already downstairs, "Good morning, Susie!"

"Good morning, Davy."

"Hey there sonny boy, how are you this morning?" Dad said as he came into the kitchen. "Who's hungry this morning?"

"What are you doing with Mom's apron on Dad?"

"Well, what do mean? I thought I would try it out, your Mom had something to do over at church this morning, so I'm in charge of breakfast."

"Are you sure, Daddy?" Susie said, with concern. "I didn't think you knew how to cook."

"Well, come on now, Susie. Of course Daddy knows how to cook. Now, who would like to have a nice big bowl of cereal this morning? Would you like the flakey ones or the popping ones? What's it going to be, eh Jelly Bean?" The kids laughed.

"Daddy, that's not cooking. Even I know how to make cereal."

"Yeah, Dad, all you need to do is put it in the bowl with some milk on top," Davy added.

"Well now, it takes some cooking skill to get it all in the bowl without making a mess. Don't you think?" Just as he splashed milk onto the table, he said, "See that hardly missed a thing."

They both let out a big laugh as they slid their bowls over.

"Okay, there we go. See that, I think I can be a chef, don't you? What do you both say about that?"

Susie said, "Daddy, you're silly," as she slurped up some of her cereal while crunching and laughing at him." "You need a little more work, Dad," Davy said. "I think you can do it if you want, but let's leave the cooking to Mom for now, okay?"

"Hahaha!" Dad laughed, "Okay, son, I think you're right. I'll need some more practice I guess. Davy and Susie finished up and grabbed their things to go to school.

"Bye, Dad. See you later!" They headed off the porch.

"See you, Daddy. Love you!"

"Love you too, Jelly Bean."

As Davy and Susie walked along, Susie turned to Davy, "So Davy, what do you think Stephen will be like today?"

"I don't know. I think he'll be all right. He seemed all right the other night."

"What are you going to say to him?"

"I'm not sure yet. I guess I'll know when the time comes, but right now, I'm not sure."

As they got a little closer to school, Taylor and Jaxson joined up with them. "Hey guys, how are you today?"

"Hey Davy, I'm still thinking about that slide we were on," Taylor said. "I even told my big brother about it!"

"Yeah, it's cool, isn't it? So, I wanted to tell you guys something before we go into school. Guess who we bumped into at Giuseppe's the other night?"

"I don't know. Who?" Jaxson asked.

"Stephen and his Mom and Dad."

"Really! What happened?"

"He came up to Susie and me and said he was sorry for being mean to us."

"Really? That doesn't sound like Stephen."

"Yeah, I know, but I think he really meant it."

"I hope so, Davy. You don't think he was just being nice because his Mom and Dad were there, do you?" Taylor said.

"Well, I really didn't think about that, but he seemed like he meant it."

"Let's hope so Davy. No one wants any more trouble from Stephen these days."

"Yeah, I know I don't."

"Me either!" Susie added.

The four finally made it to school and walked in. Susie went to her classroom and the boys went on to their own. The class was all a buzz as everyone got settled in for a new day of learning. All the seats were filling up.

Davy gave a slow turn over his shoulder to see if Stephen was at his desk. As he turned just enough to see if he was back there, Stephen walked by Davy's desk. "Hey Davy," he said.

Davy quickly turned back to see who was talking to him. He could see Stephen next to his desk. "Hey Stephen, how's it going?" That's all that came out as he sat there looking up at him.

"Okay," he said as he went on to take his seat.

Mr. Clark came into the room and gave his usual tap, tap, tap on the desk. "Okay, okay everyone. Settle down. Now before we get started, how did you all enjoy your weekend? Anyone want to tell us what their favorite part of the weekend was?" Most of the class raised their hands quickly to share.

"Okay Taylor, how about if you go first."

"All right. The best part was when I got to go over to the park with Davy and try out the slide that was there. It was awesome!"

"Well, that sounds like fun," Mr. Clark said. "I remember riding the slide at my park as a boy. Come to think of it, it was pretty awesome, too! Who would like to go next? Hmmm. Okay, Stephen, how about you?"

"Aaaahh, I had four pieces of pizza at Giuseppe's. It a new record for me, and it was really good too!"

"Well, four slices at Giuseppe's. That does sound good. You must have been pretty full after that."

"Yeah, I was really full," he replied. The kids let out a little giggle.

"Okay, we have time for one more. How about you, Davy? What was the best part of your weekend?"

"I had the chance to forgive someone this weekend. My Mom and Dad taught me that it is always a good thing when we can forgive someone."

"Davy, I would have to agree it is a good thing to forgive others and to move on from the troubles you're having. Very good. Everyone, I'm glad you all had a good weekend. Now it's time to go back in time. So let's get out our history books and turn to page 37."

As the class opened their books, Davy took another look over his shoulder. This time he could see Stephen back at his desk. Stephen looked up and waved as he was opening his book. "*Hmmm,*" Davy thought. "*I really do think he meant it.*"

So, they moved through time and history as they studied their work for the morning. The bell sounded for lunch. Davy sprang up, grabbed his lunch bag, and headed for the hall to find Taylor and Jaxson.

The three took their usual spot in the cafeteria and searched to see what was packed in their bags for lunch.

Davy opened his bag to find a peanut butter and jelly sandwich that was all crooked and had some jelly oozing from the side. It wasn't cut in nice pieces as it normally would be. Then he remembered that Dad made the lunches today and let out a little chuckle as he thought to himself, *"Oh Dad, you are quite the chef, aren't you?"*

"What's so funny, Davy?" Taylor asked.

"Oh, nothing. Just thinking of something my Dad said today." He took his sandwich from the bag and started eating when Stephen walked by their table.

"Hi Stephen, how are you doing? Would you like to sit with us for lunch today."

"Ummm. Okay." Stephen took a seat at the table with the rest of the boys and started to unpack his lunch. He had a big turkey sandwich with cheese on it.

"Wow, that's a big sandwich, Stephen," Jaxson said. "What is it?"

"Turkey and cheese."

"It looks good," Taylor said. The boys all let out a little giggle as they started to eat.

"Yeah, I like turkey," he said, as he took a big bite out of the side of his sandwich. Stephen was like a different kid, all of a sudden.

"It sure is nice to have a laugh instead of a push in the back," Davy thought. The boys ate their lunch and talked a little before the bell sounded to go back to class. They packed up their things and headed back to the classroom. The day's studies wrapped up, and the bell sounded, signaling the day had come to an end.

As the students gathered up their things to head home for the day, Stephen approached Davy. "Hey Davy, thanks for inviting me to sit at your table today for lunch. I know you really didn't have to do that, but thanks anyway."

"Yeah sure, not a problem," Davy said. "Any time."

They turned and headed off in different directions.

Davy met up with Susie, and the two started on their way home. A few minutes later, Taylor and Jaxson caught up with them.

"Hey, Davy, wait up!" Jaxson said. "What's up? We saw you talking with Stephen in the hall. Everything okay?"

"Yeah, everything is good. He just thanked me for asking him to sit at our lunch table today, that's all."

"Really? He said thank you? Stephen doesn't usually say thank you for anything."

"He did today. Maybe he's not such a bad kid after all," Taylor said.

"I don't know, I really don't know him, so I'm not going to say anything bad about him," Davy said.

"You're right Davy, maybe he is changing the way he acts and is going to be a different kind of kid from now on."

"That would be good for him and everyone else, I guess," Davy said. "We'll have to see what happens."

Susie added, "Yeah, let's see what happens. Maybe he is a good kid, and no one knows it yet."

"She could be right," Davy said, as the four kids headed towards the intersection where they normally split off and go their separate ways. "Okay, you guys, we'll see you tomorrow."

"All right, see you tomorrow, Davy."

"Bye," Susie said to the two boys, and off they went.

As Davy and Susie walked along, she looked up at her big brother and asked, "Do you think Stephen can be a different kind of boy Davy?"

"Sure I do, Susie. Anyone can change if they want to. You have to work at it, that's all."

"Work at it?" Susie said with a little puzzled look on her face. "How do you work at it?"

"I guess if you make up your mind to change something about yourself, then you really need to do your best to stick to the plan you came up with to make the change in the first place. Sometimes changing things isn't that easy, so you need to work at it. I think that's what it means anyway. We can ask Mom and Dad at dinner later. How does that sound?"

"Okay, Davy, we can work at that." The two laughed as they went along. "It's nice that Stephen is trying to be kind, don't you think?"

"Yes, it is Susie."

"Do you think that you and Stephen will be friends?"

"I'm not sure, maybe."

Chapter Ten

Think It Over

We see that Davy has a very close relationship with God, and he seems to be in conversation with God regularly.

How do you see this helping Davy in the story as he deals with things whether it's the harder things, or the fun things, or the unknown things?

_____

_____

_____

_____

_____

Even though Davy has shown many different emotions in the story, when he is scared or confused, he seems to be able to stay mostly calm or becomes calm shortly after a hard situation arises. When he was sad, he refocuses on a positive outcome. When he is happy, he is very grateful for the goodness that he experiences. God enjoys a relationship with his children.

What does your relationship with God look like?

_____

_____

_____

_____

_____

Do you talk to him through prayer?

_____

_____

     Write a prayer to God about something you are grateful for, or something that you need.

_____

_____

_____

_____

_____

_____

_____

_____

Scripture References:

1 John 3:1

"See what kind of love the Father has given to us, that we should be called children of God; and so we are."

Acts17:27

"God did this so that they would seek him and perhaps reach out for him and find him, though he is not far from any one of us."

Jeremiah 29:13

"You will seek me and find me when you seek me with all your heart."

Davy shows that forgiveness is a good thing to give to another person who has wronged you in the past. He asks Stephen if he would like to sit with him and his friends at the lunch table, hoping and having faith that Stephen was serious when he said he was sorry for what he did to him and his sister.

We talked a bit about forgiveness earlier in the story.

Can you see how this is a good thing?

_____

_____

Let's talk about how to forgive.

The act of forgiving isn't easy for some people, but did you know that God designed it to be perfect and complete?

Yes, He designed forgiveness to be lasting, and in the same way, He forgives us, we must forgive those who have hurt us as well.

By forgiving someone, you are not saying that what they did is okay, but rather, that you have decided not to hold whatever you forgive that person for against them.

It may seem unfair to just let someone off without making them pay for what they did. That is why it takes real Love to forgive — the type of Love that God has for us.

<u>Scripture Reference:</u>
Mark 11:25-26 (NIV)
"And when you stand praying, if you hold anything against anyone, forgive them, so that your Father in heaven may forgive you your sins.

But if you do not forgive, neither will your Father in heaven forgive your trespasses."

Chapter Eleven

Home Sweet Home

Susie ran just ahead of Davy as they got closer to their house. Up onto the porch, she went as she spotted her mother sitting in her favorite chair, waiting for them. "Hey, you two! How are you doing today? I missed you guys this morning. Did Dad make you a nice breakfast?"

Susie and Davy just looked at each other and giggled. "Oh, he sure did," Davy said. "Wearing your apron, he made us a bowl of cereal and splashed milk on the table."

"Yeah, Mommy, he said he was going to be the chef!"

"The chef, well, that would be nice. We can let him make all the dinners from now on. What do you guys think about that?"

"Ohhh, no, Mom! I'm not too sure about that just yet, said Davy. Dad needs way more practice, don't you think? Remember that time you asked him to make the toast for

breakfast and the whole house filled up with smoke and the siren was going off?"

"Oh, I remember that," Susie said. "That hurt my ears. It was so loud, and it made my eyes water too with all that smoke."

They all laughed out loud. "Yes, you're right, Davy. He tries hard, but can still use some practice."

"Oh good. I thought we were going to go hungry there for a while, Mom. Or maybe we can just eat cereal all the time," Susie said. "I want the ones with the marshmallows, Mommy!"

"I don't think so, Susie. I think I will just be the family chef. How's that sound?

"Sounds good to me, Mom," Davy said.

"Yeah, sounds good to me, too, Mommy."

"Speaking of dinner, I hope you are hungry because I have a nice chicken hiding in the oven, and we're going to have some biscuits, mashed potatoes, and green beans with it. What do you think about that?"

"Oh boy, that sounds good to me!" Davy rushed in and right up the steps to his bedroom, so he could do his homework before dinner was ready. The smell of biscuits baking distracted Davy from his math homework. *"Hmmm, let's see... if I had eight biscuits, and I multiplied them by eight biscuits, I would have 64 biscuits altogether."* Davy thought. *"Wow, that's a lot of biscuits! Even I don't think I can eat 64 biscuits, and I really like biscuits."*

He laughed at himself for a bit, then got back to working on his math homework. It was only a few minutes after Davy had finished, and his Mom called out for dinner. "Dinner is ready, everyone," and off he went charging down the steps.

"Whoa, whoa. Slow down there, young man. Dinner isn't going to run away, you know," Dad said as they were heading for the kitchen. The family sat at their spots around the table as Mom finished putting the last of the food on the table.

"Doesn't this look delicious?" Dad said. "I think we should give your Mom a round of applause for this meal. She really outdid herself, didn't she, Davy?"

"Oh, it sure looks like it, Dad."
They clapped their hands.

"Yay for Mommy! Now we don't have to eat cereal every night," Susie said.

"Cereal every night?" Dad said with a puzzled look on his face. "Never mind, honey, I'll tell you later," Mom said.

"Well, Davy," Dad asked. "Would you like to give thanks for our meal tonight?"

"Okay, Dad. Thank you, God, for this great food that we have to eat tonight and for my Mom being the chef in our house." Dad looked up as Mom put her hand on his and gave him a little pat. He still had that puzzled look. "And thank you, God, for all the good things that happen in our life."

"Okay, very good son," Dad said. "Let's eat. So how was everyone's day today? Susie, how about you? How was your day?"

"Good Daddy! We were reading a story."

"Oh? And what was this story about Susie?"

"It was a book about a frog and a toad even though they were different, they still became friends."

"Wow, well, that sounds pretty interesting, Susie. Do you like it so far?"

"Yes, Daddy, I do. It reminds me of Davy and Stephen. They are different, but maybe they can become friends. Davy said that if Stephen wants to be a different kind of a boy he has to work at it, is that right Daddy?"

"Yes, any time we want to make a change, we need to put effort into it. So yes. You can call that working on it, right, Davy?"

"Yeah, Dad, it seems like Stephen is looking to be nice instead of being mean to other kids, so I told Susie that he could do it if he works on it."

"That sounds right to me, and we can add that if he needs any help along the way, he should ask someone that can help out, like his mom or dad. They can give him some ideas on what to do if he gets stuck on something."

Susie chimed in, "He can say his prayers, too, right, Daddy?"

"Ohh, absolutely Susie. Saying prayers is always a good idea when we are looking to make a change and need some guidance. We can ask God for wisdom to help us through those things we are looking to change. God enjoys when we ask him for his help and thank him for being with us. That's how we do it by praying and having a relationship with him. That's something we all can keep in our mind, even for Mommy's and Daddy's Susie."

"That's right, Daddy. Maybe you can pray to be able to cook better and not burn the toast anymore."

Dad looked at Susie, "What's that, Jelly Bean?"

"Never mind, dear. I said we would talk about it later," Mom said.

They all let out a laugh at the table as they finished their dinner. Things wrapped up in the kitchen as Mom and

Dad put the last of the dishes away. Susie was coloring, and Davy was reading his book in the family room when Mom and Dad came in.

"Mom and I were talking, and we are thinking of going on a camping trip this weekend. What do you think of that?"

"A camping trip?" Davy asked.

"Yes, your Uncle Jack said that we could borrow his tent and camping gear to give it a try. If we all like it, maybe we can buy our own tent and go camping more often. What do you think about that?"

"Ahh boy, that sounds cool, Dad! You mean we sleep in the woods, have a campfire, and we can make smores?"

"Yep! We can make smores and all of that."

"Oh, but Daddy, don't bears and snakes live in the woods?" Susie asked.

"Sure they do, Susie, but they most likely aren't going to be around the camp when we get there. They like to keep to themselves, and they live a little further back in the deep woods. No need to be afraid of the bears and the snakes. We can talk more about this another time, but for now, it's time to get ready for bed."

Davy and Susie headed up the steps to get ready for bed. When they were all done getting their baths and sure to be squeaky clean, they snuggled up in their beds. Mom read Susie some of her storybook, and as her eyes became a little sleepy, she said, "Goodnight, Mommy," and closed her eyes. Mom turned off the lights, left the room, and headed for Davy's room.

"All ready for bed, Davy?"

"Yep. I'm ready, Mom," as he climbed in and pulled the covers up tight around his chin. "Mom, I'm not sure what to do about Stephen."

"No? Why do you say that, Davy? What's on your mind?"

"Well, what if he is not really a nice kid and goes back to the pushing and the teasing again?"

"Hmmm, well then, I think you will cross that bridge if it should come to that, but for now, I think you should give him a chance to show if he is serious about changing, don't you think? We really shouldn't look to make up our mind about something before we give it a chance. What if we said NO WAY! to camping just because bears and snakes live in the woods or it might rain, and we never gave it a chance? Then we would never really know the truth about how we felt about camping because we never tried it. I think we all need a chance now and then, so this is going to be up to you, but I think it may be worth your while to give him a chance."

"So, how are we doing in here?" Dad asked as he entered Davy's room.

"Mom and I were just talking about giving things a chance before we know if we would like it or not, and I think I'm going to give Stephen a chance to see if he can be a good guy."

"Okay, Davy, anytime you have a question, don't wait to ask. Mom and I are always here for you, all right?"

"Yeah, Dad, I know." Mom and Dad kissed Davy on the head and turned the light off as they left his room.

Davy closed his eyes and said, "God, I think it would be a good idea for me to give Stephen a chance to show if he is ready to change and be a good guy towards other kids. Can you give him some help, God while he is changing? I hope we can be friends someday."

Chapter Eleven
Think It Over

We have all been given many talents and gifts in our life from our heavenly Father, but the most exclusive gift he has given us from all of the rest of creation is the gift of free will. The ability to make our own choices can bring great satisfaction and achievement, but it can also get us in some trouble as well. When we make choices that are in line with the teaching of Jesus, we can rest easy that we are doing the right things in our life.

We hear Davy talking at dinner about the **choice** that Stephen has made to try harder to be nice to other kids and not bully them around. They are also discussing what it takes to **change**. Sometimes when we try to change a behavior, it can be a bit challenging, and we need to put in a good effort to make that change happen. We can also get support from people in our life who love us and want to help us be the best version of ourselves, and let's not forget Susie's suggestion to pray because God is our biggest fan and Jesus is always available to hear our prayers and the Holy Spirit is the helper above all helpers!

What are some of the changes that happened in Davy's life through the story?

_____

_____

_____

_____

_____

What examples of change can you identify in your own life up until now?

_____

_____

_____

_____

_____

Do you think at some point you may have treated someone unfairly or even bullied them?

_____

_____

If so what do you feel you can change in order not to repeat those behaviors and to be more kind towards others?

_____

_____

_____

_____

_____

Do you feel you have the strength in your heart to give someone a chance to change and what would that look like to you?

_____

_____

_____

_____

_____

<u>Scripture References:</u>
Philippians 4:6-7

"Do not be anxious about anything, but in every situation, by prayer and petition, with thanksgiving, present your request to God. And the peace of God, which transcends all

understanding, will guard your hearts and your minds in

Christ Jesus."

Romans 9:28

"And we know that in all things God works for the good of
those who love him, who have been called according to his
purpose."

Chapter Twelve

Change Is In The Air

Davy woke up to the sound of his alarm clock. He got out of bed and noticed that it was a little cooler than usual. So he reached over to close his window. *"I guess it's time to get ready for another day of school,"* he thought. Since he was already a pro at getting ready for school, he went right into his routine. Brush teeth, wash face, fix hair, make bed, get dressed, one by one until he was ready for breakfast. This time he was waiting at the table for his sister to show up.

"Hey," Susie said. "You beat me to the table today, Davy."

"Yep! I'm pretty fast at getting ready now that I have my routine down. I think I'm going to be first from now on."

"It's not a race. I like to take my time when I'm brushing my hair, and your hair isn't as long as mine, you know. So my hair takes a little longer I guess."

"Now, now, you two. No one said it had to be a race. We just need to make sure we are done, and on time when that bell rings at school, okay?"

"All right, Mommy. What are we having for breakfast today?"

"I thought today we would have...taaadaa! Pancakes!"

"Aahhh, my favorite," Davy said. "Do they have bananas in them?"

"Yep! They do," Mom said. "I thought I would make up for yesterday's ordinary breakfast with a special one this morning."

Davy said, "Dad can make us cereal more often if it means we get pancakes the next day, Mom!"

"Yeah, Mom," Susie said. "I can go for that too. Cereal, pancakes, cereal, pancakes; that works for me! Davy, go ahead and say grace before we eat. I'm hungry."

"Thank you, God, for all the great things you bring my family and all that you do in our lives. Please continue to help us with the hard stuff that pops up from time to time. Amen!"

Both Davy and Susie gobbled up their pancakes in no time, got themselves cleaned up, and were ready to head out the door for another day of school. They put on their backpacks and said good-bye to Mom as she came into the foyer. She opened the door for them and said, "Hmmm. It's a little chilly this morning. Maybe you should put on a sweater."

"Okay, Mommy. Can I wear my pink one?"

"Sure, Susie. How about your camo sweatshirt Davy?"

"Okay, Mom." Off they went, now that they had their warm sweaters on.

"The leaves on the trees will be changing soon, Susie."

"Yeah, I wonder if they have a pumpkin patch around here," she said. "Carving pumpkins is fun, isn't it, Davy?"

"Yeah, I want to make a Batman pumpkin this year."

"I'm going to make one with a big smile on his face," said Susie. "And he is going to wear a hat."

"A hat?"

"Yeah, I'm going to borrow one of Daddy's hats to keep his head warm while he sits out on the porch." Davy let out a laugh as they were heading toward their school. When they got to the intersection, Taylor and Jaxson were waiting for them.

"Hi guys, how are you doing today?" Jaxson yelled out.

"Hi!" Davy said, "Are you ready for the history test today?"

"Yeah. I studied last night, and my mom asked me some practice questions," Taylor said.

"That's a good idea," Davy said. "I never thought about that. I just read the chapter over, but I think I'm going to get a 100 on this one."

"Davy, are you going to ask Stephen if he wants to sit at our lunch table again today?"

"I don't know. I haven't really thought about it. It just kind of happened yesterday. What do you guys think?"

"I don't mind. I think Stephen was nice yesterday."

"I don't mind either," said Jaxson. "Maybe we can get to know him better if we give him a chance, now that he's being a nice guy."

"I think that's a good idea," said Davy. "Everyone should get a chance to show they can be a better person. So, if we see Stephen at lunch, we can ask him if he would like to sit with us, right?"

"Yep," said Taylor and Jaxson.

"Okay, then, let's do it."

The four students got to the front doors of the school and went straight to their classrooms. Susie turned down the hall and waved to Davy and the boys as she went into hers. Davy entered the room and set his things on the shelf, hung up his sweatshirt, and headed to his desk. As everyone got themselves situated at their desk, Mr. Clark entered the room.

"Good morning, everyone. How are we doing today?" He said. "I hope you all made a good effort with studying for your exam. This is your first big test of the year. Is everyone excited?"

"Yeahhh!" The class yelled out.

"That doesn't sound like a lot of excitement to me. Let's try that again. Does everyone feel excited about taking their first big test today?"

"Yesss, Mr. Clark!"

"Now that's more like it. We've got some excitement in the air today, students! Okay, I am going to hand out your test. I don't want you to flip them over until I say so, all right? Everyone understand?"

Davy was confident that he was going to do well on this test since he put in some extra time studying. After Mr. Clark finished getting all the tests passed out, he gave a couple more instructions to follow and then allowed the students to get started. Davy read the questions carefully, and one by one, the answers popped into his head. He was feeling pretty good about getting a good grade on it when he finished.

As everyone finished up and handed their test back to Mr. Clark, Davy sat at his desk, waiting patiently. When all the completed tests were handed back to Mr. Clark, he said, "Okay, very good, everyone. You all finished on time, so I am going to give you a short 10-minute break. If anyone needs to use the restroom or get a drink, you can quietly get up from your seat and do so. Remember, only 10 minutes, then we all need to be sitting back in our seats."

Davy thought, "*Hmmm, maybe I'll grab a drink. That test made me thirsty*". He got up from his seat and went to the water fountain, took a couple of sips, and turned to go back to his desk. As he turned around he bumped right into Stephen, who was standing just behind him.

"Oh, I'm sorry," Davy said. "I didn't know anyone was standing behind me."

"It's okay. I think you just stepped on my toes Davy, no big deal."

"Okay, enjoy your drink," he said to Stephen and went back to his desk.

Davy didn't know what else to say at that moment, so he just sat at his desk. He did start to wonder if he should have said more or even asked Stephen if he would like to have lunch with him and the other boys this afternoon. He wasn't sure how to handle that since Stephen did have some other boys he hung around with, and the girl named Megan. These were the same kids who always laughed when Stephen made fun of Davy and called him a Pirate.

Davy asked, *"So, what should I do about this God? How should I handle this? I can sure use some help to figure all this out."*

The tap came from Mr. Clark's desk as he called out for everyone to take their seats. "All right, all right. Everyone settle down now. I hope you enjoyed your little break. It's time to move on with our studies. Let's take out our math books and open up to page 53."

Everyone opened their books. The clunk of the books on the desks and the ruffle of the pages turning was all Davy could hear. Then one quick moment, it all went quiet. Davy thought, *"I'll invite them too. Why not? The table is big enough for everyone."* He knew that was the right thing to do. *"Be friends with as many kids as you can. Anyone who wants to sit at the table is welcome."* He felt in his heart that this was the right way to think. After he was satisfied with his decision, his focus redirected back to class and what Mr. Clark was teaching.

Studies moved along until the lunch bell rang. Everyone jumped to their feet and scattered to grab their things. Davy entered the hall, met up with Taylor and Jaxson, and headed off to the cafeteria for lunch. They got to the table where they normally sat and opened up their lunches. It wasn't long before Stephen was walking in the area of their table.

When Davy spotted him. He said, "Hey, Stephen. Would you like to sit with us again today?"

"Sure, I guess. Why not?" Stephen took a seat with the boys as they started digging into their lunch bags.

"Hey Davy, what do you have today?" Taylor asked.

"I'm not sure, but I do see a chocolate pudding cup."

"Oh boy, I love pudding cups! Davy, do you want to trade? I have an apple."

"Hahaha! No way. It's not every day I get chocolate pudding. But I'll let you have some."

"Really?" Taylor said. "Nah, that's okay. I'll ask my Mom if she can buy some the next time she goes to the store. But thanks anyway, I totally understand. I don't think I could give up my chocolate pudding either, Davy."

So they took out their lunch and started talking about the test they took and some other things. Davy mentioned that his family was going to be going on a camping trip. Stephen added that he and his parents went on a camping trip to the mountains and stayed in a cabin at the lake. He was telling everyone at the table how much fun they all had when they went canoeing, swimming, and he even talked about their big campfire. They all were really having a nice talk.

Then, Ricky, Megan, and Brian came by. They were the ones Stephen hung around with, the same kids who were laughing at Davy when Stephen was teasing him. "Hey Stephen, what are you doing sitting here with the Pirate? Are you going to be a Pirate too? Maybe we can get you a big black pirate hat and a patch to go along with it. What do think?"

Stephen didn't say a word, and neither did anyone else sitting at the table. Stephen stood up and looked at the boys as they laughed at their own comments. They both looked up at Stephen. Ricky and Brian forgot how big he was and who they were making fun of. The look on their faces soon changed from a smile to a look of great concern. The table was so quiet you could hear their hearts beating as they stood there.

"Oh boy," they said. "What did we do?"

After a moment, Stephen reached out his hand to shake with Ricky and said, "Guys, that's it. We're not going to be teasing and picking on kids anymore. That's not the right thing to do. I learned that it's not what God wants from us. I learned from my Mom and Dad that the Bible says we should love one another as Jesus loves us. It doesn't say we should push kids around or call them nasty names. So now, if I get angry with someone for what they say or do, I do my best to think of Jesus instead of being mean to them or trying to get back at them. And I know now that if I need help, I can go and ask for it. It's okay to ask for help when you need it. These guys are pretty cool, and I like them. And it's just not nice to try to give other kids a hard time. I'm done with that, and I hope you are too."

Ricky and Brian looked at each other. The other boys still sat there, waiting to see what they were going to say next. Then Ricky opened up and said, "Okay Stephen, that sounds good to me. I never really liked picking on kids anyway."

With a big smile, Davy said, "Why don't you guys sit with us at our table? We've got lots of room."

So they did. The kids all joined in and shared their lunchtime stories and laughed with each other. And just like that, they learned a very valuable lesson. One that they will carry with them the rest of the school year and beyond. Kindness is so much better than being mean, and love will always be better than hate. It's just not cool to say mean things to other kids because of how they look or where they come from or for any reason.

Other students from their class joined in as word spread of Stephen's transformation from big and nasty to kindness. They wanted to be part of this new group of friends and to see what this was all about. Soon the lunchroom became a closer place as others wanted to sit with Davy and his friends. They even had to move some tables together to make room for everyone who would come to join them and take part in what was happening.

Over the course of the year, Davy, Taylor and Jaxson, started a club, and anyone who wanted to join had to agree to stand against bullying and watch out for one another. Their mission was to report bullying wherever they saw it happen, whether it was on the playground, in the park, or on the field and even on the internet. It didn't matter where. Their motto became, TOGETHER WE CAN END BULLYING!! That's what they were all about. Soon other moms and dads, teachers, and coaches were joining their efforts as well. It seemed as if everyone wanted to help.

That year Davy became a hero in his community as he sought to learn and teach others more about bullying, signs of bullying, and how to stop it. He was even asked to speak about their club at other schools in the area. His friends all helped tell their story altogether and the efforts continued to grow beyond what they could ever imagine.

ARE YOU READY TO END BULLYING IN YOUR SCHOOL??

Join Davy and his friends and find out how you can become part of the solution instead of being part of the problem!

Chapter 12

Think It Over

In this chapter, Stephen's old friends, who were used to being around him when he would bully kids around, approached him and tried to continue the bullying. This time they tried to bully Stephen and were teasing him. That didn't last long, and Stephen did something unexpected; he showed some real change as he didn't fight back, but instead showed a great example of how you can change from bad to good.

As he stood up to the bullying and suggested kindness instead, which he learned through changing himself, that love and kindness are better choices than being mean and hurtful towards others. Jesus teaches us in his word that we should love others as he loves us and that we should love each other as we love ourselves.

Let's talk about what that means in our life.

Jesus says we should love each other as he loves us. Talk about how Jesus loved us. Can you give some examples of how Jesus loves us?

_____

_____

_____

_____

_____

Examples such as he healed our wounds, our illness, our hunger, and, most importantly our souls through his sacrifice on the cross for our sins.

Davy suggested that the others sit at their table as well, and many more joined afterward. Davy felt all the kids in the lunchroom were welcome to join in, and through their great effort, they changed the way people in their school and community thought about bullying, and they became more aware of bullying and the signs of bullying and what they should do to prevent it.

This new attitude was a big change in their school. How do you think you may be able to make even a little change in your surroundings to stop bullying and to spread love and kindness to others?

_____

_____

_____

_____

_____

What positive things can make other people feel more comfortable in their school environment, on a sports team, or the playground?

_____

_____

_____

_____

_____

Think of some things that you would like to do for others or what you may want someone to do for you.

_____

_____

_____

_____

_____

Thank you for reading this story and participating in "Think it Over."

My prayer is that as young children, we can learn the difference between love and kindness vs. hate and meanness.

As adults, we can lead by example to teach children who are entrusted to you. And to raise them according to the will of God and the teaching of Jesus Christ.

Amen and God Bless you.

Leader

And

Parent Guide

Chapter One

Study Guide Questions

How did Davy feel when he first found out he and his family were going to be moving away, and all his plans were going to change unexpectedly? **Sad.**

Discuss how you might feel if you were Davy.

_____

_____

_____

How did Davy's attitude change as he watched his friends from the back window of his Dad's car?

He became more comfortable and had faith in God's plan.

Do you think you can be like Davy?

_____

_____

How?

_____

_____

_____

Scripture References:

Proverbs 3: 5-6

Trust in the Lord with all your heart and lean not on your own understanding; in all ways, submit to him, and he will make your paths straight.

Romans 8: 28

And we know that in all things God works for the good of those who love him, who have been called according to his purpose.

Chapter Two

Study Guide Questions

The family showed some examples of love for one another, can you name two examples that you see?

Davy's Mom made his favorite breakfast, Davy holding his sister's hand on the way to school. Davy helped his sister to her classroom and waited for her after school.

Did Stephen show love or kindness towards Davy on his first day at school? **No**

How could Stephen have shown Davy some love or kindness on his first day of school, instead of being mean to him and hurting his feelings?

Discuss some options. Such as showing him around his new school, introducing him to some of the other students, inviting him to join at his lunch table.

Scripture References:

Matthew 22: 37: 39

Jesus replied "Love the Lord God with all your heart and with all your soul and with all your mind. This is the first and greatest commandment. And the second is like it: Love your neighbor as yourself.

1 Corinthians 13: 13

"so now faith, hope, and love abide, these three; but the greatest of these is love."

Chapter Three

Study Guide Questions

The family often gives thanks to God in the story. What can you find in your life to give God thanks for? **Have a discussion of the importance of being grateful for these things.**

Are there people or things in your life that you can say you're grateful for? List 3

_____

_____

_____

<u>Scripture References:</u>

1 Thessalonians 5:18

Give thanks in all circumstances; for this is God's will for you in Christ Jesus.

Psalm 106:1

Praise the Lord. Give thanks to the Lord for he is good; his love endures forever

Davy seemed to be confused about how to handle things at school. What do you think you would have done if you were Davy? **Discuss some suitable options.**

It is important to report bullying. There is a difference between tattling on someone and telling someone like a teacher or parent about something that is going on that you believe is wrong or hurtful.

- **Tattling is reporting to an adult about someone else's behavior to get them in trouble.**

- **Telling is reporting to a responsible adult about someone else's behavior to help someone – themselves or someone else.**

Children need to understand how important it is to report bullying. Parents can help by encouraging children to talk about what is happening at school, in their neighborhoods, on the bus, etc.

Give an example of when you might have "tattled" on someone.

_____

_____

_____

How did you feel after tattling?

_____

_____

_____

Have you ever told a responsible adult about something that happened to help someone else?

_____

_____

How did you feel after telling?

_____

_____

_____

<u>Scripture Reference:</u>

Psalm 46: 1

God is our refuge and strength, an ever-present help in trouble.

Chapter Four

Study Guide Questions

Stephen continues to bully and give Davy a hard time, and now he is even bullying Susie and calling her names. Bullying can be very difficult; we see Davy tell Stephen to stop! Do you think this was a good idea?

Yes

Why?

_____

_____

_____

How would you have handled the situation?

_____

_____

_____

Tell the bully to stop. Again, bullies often do not expect someone to stand up to them. In fact, they often target kids who they believe they can intimidate. As a result, telling a bully to stop in a strong and confident voice can be very effective.

Bullies often count on finding a victim who will not say anything at all. But if your child makes sure the bully knows he cannot walk all over him, the bully is more likely to stop what he is doing.

Are you courageous enough to stand up to someone who is bullying you or a friend?

_____

_____

Do you believe God is always with you?

_____

_____

Is there something you can share about Him being with you in a time of trouble?

_____

_____

_____

Scripture References:

Luke 17: 3

"If your brother or sister sins against you, rebuke them and if they repent, forgive them."

Joshua 1:9

"Have I not commanded you? Be strong and courageous. Do not be afraid; do not be discouraged, for the LORD your God will be with you wherever you go."

Chapter Five

Study Guide Questions

Susie and the family sit down for dinner, and Susie speaks right up as she often does and reports the morning bullying to her mom and dad, was she right for doing this? **Yes.**

Why?

_____

_____

_____

Report the bullying to an adult. Be sure your child knows that the best way to prevent bullying is to report it. Without adult intervention, bullying will often continue or escalate.

Talk about the reasons why kids don't tell others they are being bullied and be sure your children know that you understand their fears.

Stress that while it takes a lot of strength and courage to report bullying, it is the smartest way to handle this type of situation. Also, be careful not to engage in victim-blaming or to criticize your child for

getting bullied. Bullying is a choice made by the bully and never the responsibility of the victim.

Scripture Reference:

Proverbs 22: 6

Start children off on the way they should go, and even when they are old, they will not turn from it.

That evening Davy prays for Stephen so that whatever is bothering him may come out, and he can get over the thing that is upsetting him and causing him to act badly towards others.

Do you think that God wants us to pray for people like Stephen? **Yes.**

Why should we pray for people who hurt us? Kids bully for many reasons. Some bully because they feel insecure. Picking on someone who seems emotionally or physically weaker provides a feeling of being more important, popular, or in control. In other cases, kids bully because they simply don't know that it's unacceptable to pick on kids who are different because of size, looks, race, or religion.

Scripture References:

Luke 23:34

Jesus said, "Father forgive them, for they do not know what they are doing," And they divided up his clothes by casting lots.

Matthew 5:44

But I tell you to love your enemies and pray for anyone who mistreats you.

Chapter Six

Study Guide Questions

Davy's friends are beginning to show support for their new friend.

Do you think it is important to have friends to help stand against bullies or maybe be a friend to someone who is being bullied? **Yes.**

Have a discussion about having friends and being a good friend.

- **Stick with friends.**
- **Bullies usually look for kids who are alone or socially isolated.**
- **Be sure your child knows that hanging out with friends is a great way to prevent bullying.**
- **If your child struggles with social skills or has very few friends, take steps to help him develop friendships.**
- **Having just one healthy friendship can go a long way in protecting your child from bullies.**

Scripture Reference:

Philippians 2:4

"Let each of you look not only to his own interest, but also to the interest of others."

Davy and Susie discuss forgiveness; do you believe forgiveness is important? Why?

_____

_____

_____

Discuss the benefits and importance of forgiveness.

Scripture Reference:

Matthew 6: 14-15

For if you forgive other people when they sin against you, your heavenly Father will also forgive you. But if you do not forgive others their sins, your Father will not forgive your sins.

Chapter Seven

Study Guide Questions

Davy shows us that he really relies on God to direct his day, and he does this by praying to God and having heartfelt conversation.

Do you think this can help you in your day?

_____

_____

How?

_____

_____

_____

Why do you think prayer is important?

_____

_____

_____

Have a conversation about the importance of prayer.

Mr. Clark plays a big role in the intervention process and understands that bullying is a serious issue. If your child or someone you know is being bullied at school, it is important to address the situation with the school teacher and administrators so that the situation can be resolved quickly and with as little damage as possible.

Message for parents:

Educators play a vital role not only in bullying prevention but also in bullying intervention.

In fact, helping victims through a bullying ordeal helps solidify that child's future academic success and overall well-being. But for some educators, knowing exactly what to do or say can seem overwhelming at times. After all, teachers are not trained to serve as counselors. Their job is to educate. But they can support the overall recovery process in the classroom and incorporate it into the daily learning schedule.

Bullying can be very emotional, so speaking calmly and appropriately with the school administrators is a very important step in the process.

Scripture Reference:
Romans 15: 5
"Now, the God of patience and consolation grant you to be like-minded one toward another according to Christ Jesus."

Davy showed a tremendous amount of understanding for Stephen when he learned Stephen was bullied at his past school and is even willing to help Stephen.

How do you see Davy's actions towards the person who was picking on him?

_____

_____

_____

Have a discussion on empathy (*The ability to understand and share the feelings of another*).

Can you give an example of a time when you felt empathy for someone?

_____

_____

_____

Message for parents.

One of the most complicated types of bullying to address is that of bully-victims. Bully-victims represent kids who are both bullies and victims. They bully others because they, too, have been bullied.

Because bully-victims face a complicated set of consequences, it is essential that parents and others recognize the challenges they face and design interventions to match their needs. For instance, these kids may benefit from programs that focus on cognitive restructuring, problem-solving, conflict resolution, and emotions management.

Scripture Reference:

2 Corinthians 1 3:4

"Blessed be the God and Father of our Lord Jesus Christ, the Father of mercies and God of all comfort, who comforts us in all our affliction, so that we may be able to comfort those who are in any affliction, with the comfort with which we ourselves are comforted by God."

Chapter Eight
Study Guide Questions

The new friends are really starting to form a bond of true friendship. Friends are important in our life's journey.

Parents <u>please</u> teach your children that human beings were created to be social creatures, meaning that we are most comfortable when we have family, friends, and acquaintances.

Friendship is an important element in a fulfilled, contented life, and those who have close friends, whether one or two or a multitude, will usually be happy and well adjusted.

Friends can, at times, cause us grief and hardship, but they mostly have a positive influence in our life; friends can console and help us when we are in trouble or in need of support.

Can you think of a time when a friend was there to help you through a tough time?

_____

_____

Give an example of a time you were there to help a friend in need.

_____

_____

_____

The book of Proverbs gives us wisdom for navigating the complexities of our relationships. And more specifically, friendships, even what to look for in a true friend.

Scripture References:

Proverbs 13:20

"He who walks with the wise grows wise, but a companion of fools suffers harms."

Proverbs 27:17

"As iron sharpens iron, so one man sharpens another."

Proverbs 18:24

"One who has unreliable friends soon comes to ruin, but there is a friend who sticks closer than a brother."

Chapter Nine

Study Guide Questions

In this chapter, we see the two boys arrive at an unexpected meeting, one that could have been very uncomfortable for everyone, children, and parents alike, but instead, it turns out to be a step in a new direction for the two boys.

God often uses bad or uncomfortable things or situations to bring good or healing to a situation.

How might you have felt if you were Davy?

_____

_____

Now, change things up; think of how you may have felt if you were Stephen.

_____

_____

_____

Have a discussion as if you were in the story first from Davys view then Stephens view and even try from being the parents.

Scripture Reference:

Ephesians 4:32

"Be kind to one another, tenderhearted, forgiving one another, as God in Christ forgave you."

Stephen has come to an understanding of what he did was wrong, and wants to apologize for his actions.

How do you feel when you understand that your action was the wrong thing to do?

Have a discussion on admitting wrong doing and asking for forgiveness.

Scripture Reference:

1 John 1:9

"If we confess our sins, he is faithful and just to forgive us our sins and to cleanse us from all unrighteousness."

We hear Davy comment on how things worked out just as he had hoped and prayed for, that the two can just be nice to one and other. It's a wonderfully spiritual feeling when God answers our prayers.

Can you think of a time when God answered a prayer in your life?

_____

_____

_____

And how did that make you feel?

_____

_____

_____

<u>Scripture Reference:</u>

John 15:7

"if you abide in me, and my words abide in you, ask whatever you wish, and it will be done for you."

Chapter Ten

Study Guide Questions

We see that Davy has a very close relationship with God, and he seems to be in conversation with God regularly.

How do you see this helping Davy in the story as he deals with things whether it's the harder things, or the fun things, or the unknown things?

_____

_____

_____

Even though Davy has shown many different emotions in the story when he is scared or confused, he seems to be able to stay mostly calm or becomes calm shortly after a hard situation arises. When he was sad, he refocused on a positive outcome. When he is happy, he is very grateful for the goodness that he experiences. God enjoys relationship with his children.

What does your relationship with God look like?

_____

_____

Do you talk to him through prayer?

_____

_____

_____

Invite a discussion about prayer and its importance in the lives of all of God's children, no matter how young or old.

Write a prayer to God about something you are grateful for, or something that you need.

_____

_____

_____

<u>Scripture References:</u>
1 John 3:1
"See what kind of love the Father has given to us, that we should be called children of God; and so we are.

Acts17:27
"God did this so that they would seek him and perhaps reach out for him and find him, though he is not far from any one of us."

Jeremiah 29:13

"You will seek me and find me when you seek me with all your heart."

Davy shows that forgiveness is a good thing to give to another person who has wronged you in the past. He asks Stephen if he would like to sit with him and his friends at the lunch table, hoping and having faith that Stephen was serious when he said he was sorry for what he did to him and his sister.

We talked a bit about forgiveness earlier in the story.

Can you see how this is a good thing?

_____

_____

Lets talk about how to forgive.

The act of forgiving isn't easy for some people, but did you know that God designed it to be perfect and complete?

Yes, He designed forgiveness to be lasting, and in the same way He forgives us, we must forgive those who have hurt us as well.

By forgiving someone, you are not saying that what they did is okay, but rather, that you have decided not to hold whatever you forgive that person for against them.

It may seem unfair to just let someone off without making them pay for what they did. That is why it takes real Love to forgive — the type of Love that God has for us.

Scripture Reference:
Mark 11:25,26

"And whenever you stand praying, if you have anything against anyone, forgive him, that your Father in heaven may also forgive you your trespasses.
But if you do not forgive, neither will your Father in heaven forgive your trespasses."

Chapter Eleven

Study Guide Questions

We have all been given many talents and gifts in our life from our heavenly Father, but the most exclusive gift he has given us from all of the rest of creation is the gift of free will. The ability to make our own choices can bring great satisfaction and achievement, but it can also get us in some trouble as well. When we make choices that are in line with the teaching of Jesus, we can rest easy that we are doing the right things in our life.

We hear Davy talking at dinner about the **choice** that Stephen has made to try harder to be nice to other kids and not bully them around. They are also discussing what it takes to **change**. Sometimes when we try to change a behavior it can be a bit challenging, and we need to put in a good effort to make that change happen. We can also get support from people in our life who love us and want to help us be the best version of ourselves, and let's not forget Susie's suggestion to pray because God is our biggest fan and Jesus is always available to hear our prayers and the Holy Spirit is the helper above all helpers!

Have a discussion about change using some points relative to the story.

- Davy and his family changed the place where they lived
- Summer plans with Jimmy and Cooper were changed because
- Davy's dad changed jobs and the family had to move so,
- Davy and Susie had to change schools

Discuss some of the feelings that came along with those changes, both positive and not so great for Davy.

As part of the discussion talk about how God's plan always works for the good of those who believe (Romans 8:28).

- Davy didn't want to leave Jimmy and Cooper but he found great friends in Taylor and Jaxson.
- After Stephen received some good guidance from his family and caring adults at the school, he realized he wasn't acting in a way that was appropriate or pleasing to God.

- **Davy had hoped there would be a calm between him and Stephen, but God had a plan that the boys would become friends.**

What examples of change can you identify in your own life up until now?

_____

_____

_____

Do you think at some point you may have treated someone unfairly or even bullied them?

_____

_____

If so what do you feel you can change in order not to repeat those behaviors and to be more kind towards others?

_____

_____

_____

Do you feel you have the strength in your heart to give someone a chance to change and what would that look like to you?

_____

_____

_____

Scripture References:
Philippians 4:6-7

"Do not be anxious about anything, but in every situation, by prayer and petition, with thanksgiving, present your request to God. And the peace of God, which transcends all understanding, will guard your hearts and your minds in Christ Jesus."

Romans 8:28

"And we know that in all things God works for the good of those who love him, who have been called according to his purpose."

Chapter Twelve
Study Guide Questions

In this chapter, Stephen's old friends, who were used to being around him when he would bully kids around approached him and tried to continue the bullying. This time they tried to bully Stephen, and were teasing him. That didn't last long, but Stephen did something unexpected and showed some real change as he didn't fight back, but instead showed a great example of how you can change from bad to good.

As he stood up to the bullying and suggested kindness instead, which he learned through changing himself, that love and kindness are better choices than being mean and hurtful towards others. Jesus teaches us in his word that we should love others as he loves us and that we should love each other as we love ourselves.

Let's talk about what that means in our life.

Jesus says we should love each other as he loves us. Talk about how Jesus loved us. Can you give some examples of how Jesus loves us?

_____

_____

_____

Examples such as he healed our wounds, our illness, our hunger and, most importantly our souls through his sacrifice on the cross for our sins.

Davy suggested that the others sit at their table as well, and many more joined afterward. Davy felt all the kids in the lunchroom were welcome to join in, and through their great effort they changed the way people in their school and community thought about bullying, and they became more aware of bullying and the signs of bullying and what they should do to prevent it.

This new attitude was a big change in their school. How do you think you may be able to make even a little change in your surroundings to stop bullying and to spread love and kindness to others?

_____

_____

_____

Discuss positive things that can make other people feel more comfortable in their school environment, on a sports team, or the playground.

Think of some things that you would like to do for others or even what you may want someone to do for you.

_____

_____

_____

A Note About the Author

James "Jim" Coleman, is blessed to be the father of three grown children. As a parent, he knows raising children is not always easy, especially in these trying times. There are always ups, downs, challenges, and triumphs.

Jim says:

"This story came to me during one of those challenging times, and God tugged at my heart to complete it. *Davy Meets His Goliath* offers an opportunity to build relationships with your children and open communication that is essential to all good relationships. Having forgiveness in our hearts is so very important because, at some point, we all fall short. When we do, love and kindness will be needed to be able to forgive completely. That is the message I was given by God to share with you through this story.

"In building the best foundation for our children, we can nourish that good relationship with the love of Christ so all of God's good plans can pour into the heart of what we pass on to this world, a child of God, a true follower of Jesus Christ.

"I hope that the heart of God within you and me as poured out onto these pages brings joy to all who read this story because joy can be found in all of it... if you just know where to look."

Be sure to visit: www.davymeetshisgoliath.com and www.togetherwecanendbullying.com

www.togetherwecanendbullying.com

Made in the USA
Middletown, DE
28 August 2020